Trans Affirming Churches

of related interest

God, Gender, Sex and Marriage
Mandy Ford
ISBN 978 1 78592 475 0
eISBN 978 1 78450 860 9

The Role of Religion in Peacebuilding
Crossing the Boundaries of Prejudice and Distrust
Edited by Pauline Kollontai, Sue Yore and Sebastian Kim
ISBN 978 1 78592 336 4
eISBN 978 1 78450 657 5

The A-Z of Gender and Sexuality
From Ace to Ze
Morgan Lev Edward Holleb
ISBN 978 1 78592 342 5
eISBN 978 1 78450 663 6

Everything You Ever Wanted to Know about Trans (But Were Afraid to Ask)
Brynn Tannehill
ISBN 978 1 78592 826 0
eISBN 978 1 78450 956 9

Trans Affirming Churches
How to Celebrate Gender-Variant People and Their Loved Ones

CHRISTINA BEARDSLEY
and
CHRIS DOWD

Foreword by Dr Susannah Cornwall

Jessica Kingsley Publishers
London and Philadelphia

Poem in Appendix D is reproduced with kind permission
of Performance Activist Peterson Toscano.

First published in 2020
by Jessica Kingsley Publishers
73 Collier Street
London N1 9BE, UK
and
400 Market Street, Suite 400
Philadelphia, PA 19106, USA

www.jkp.com

Library of Congress Cataloging in Publication Data
A CIP catalog record for this book is available from the Library of Congress

British Library Cataloguing in Publication Data
A CIP catalogue record for this book is available from the British Library

ISBN 978 1 78592 532 0
eISBN 978 1 78450 925 5

Printed and bound in the United States

Dedicated to all the trans people, their loved ones and allies, who have assisted us in writing this book,

and to the memory of

Canon Arthur Russell Millbourn, and other pioneers of transgender people's spiritual care.

'As a mum you want to bring them in and wrap them up and you be the refuge, but surely there should be a church that is their refuge, surely, but there now I am sure there is [where she currently resides].' (Becky, mother of a transgender daughter)

'What would help would be for people to stop being judgemental. This is the first and most important step and I would say that people claim not to be judgemental but with a careful...prodding they reveal their actual thoughts.' (George, trans man)

'My ideal minister is one that is probably much like the ones I have now that are willing to listen and talk to me about trans theology and how it helps me sort of discuss it so I don't go off on some giant heretical slant... To be able...to be willing to publicly say that they are trans accepting...willing to give trans people a voice where trans people don't have a voice...willing to use their position to advocate for trans inclusion.' (Steve, trans man)

Contents

Foreword

This is a practical, accessible, user-friendly book, the fruit of the authors' many years of experience working with trans people negotiating their relationships with religious institutions and communities of faith. As the title suggests, you have in your hands a no-nonsense how-to guide, both for churches already certain they want to fully nurture and support their trans members (and welcome new ones) and for those which are dipping a toe in the water and just want to learn more. I am delighted that it is appearing now, following a period of immense scrutiny of trans people both within the Church and in society more widely.

A lack of good-quality spiritual care for people exploring or undergoing gender transition, or who have transitioned some years before, continues to exacerbate the difficulties many gender-variant people face. In my own work, most recently the Modelling Transgender Spiritual Care project, funded by the Sir Halley Stewart Trust and conducted in partnership with the West of England NHS Specialist Gender Identity Clinic, it has become clear to me that at a time when gender healthcare services are under unprecedented pressure and waiting times are spiralling (with many people now waiting several years for initial appointments), communities of faith have an important role to play in supporting and upholding trans people and their families (Cornwall, forthcoming 2019). I am so pleased that Christina Beardsley and Chris Dowd have developed such a valuable resource which has potential to go a long way in making this happen.

Christina is a former trustee for trans people of Changing Attitude England, and a long-standing member of Sibyls, the Christian spirituality group for trans people, their families and supporters. She has written extensively on Christian responses to trans people, and I first became aware of her work when I read her incisive and devastating critique (2005) of the Church of England's Archbishops' Council 2003 document *Some Issues in Human Sexuality*. Christina, herself a Church of England priest, noted that the document's chapter on transgender discounted psychological and other scientific insights about trans identity, and anthropological insights about gender variance in other cultures; failed to draw on trans people's own experience, including that of social and religious ostracisation; advocated misgendering people; and failed to interrogate its own use of the Bible. Christina's other previous work, like this new book, testifies to her deep commitment to facilitating trans inclusion in profoundly practical ways: it includes *The Transsexual Person Is My Neighbour: Pastoral Guidelines for Christian Clergy, Pastors and Congregations* (2007); *This is My Body: Hearing the Theology of Transgender Christians* (2016), a collection of writings by Sibyls members co-edited by Michelle O'Brien; and, with Chris Dowd and Justin Tanis, *Transfaith: A Transgender Pastoral Resource* (2018).

Chris, a United Reformed Church minister, is a cisgender man whose work with trans people of faith has been motivated by a desire to create and promote better pastoral responses. His doctoral thesis from the University of Birmingham, which I had the privilege of examining, used participatory research and indigenous knowledge to engage in depth with trans people's experiences of church membership and belonging, and the insights that their own self-understanding had allowed them with regard to theological and biblical accounts of gender and sex. It became the basis for the 2018 *Transfaith* book. Subsequently, in collaboration with Christina, Chris has run workshops for churches and other community groups on trans spirituality and inclusion, and he has spoken widely on trans and faith in the UK and Australia.

Christina's and Chris's experiences of ministry, both in congregations and chaplaincy settings and within support networks, have given them a depth of understanding of the hurt and bemusement often felt by trans people who have found churches less nurturing places than they had hoped. This book is a concrete, realistic, hands-on response. It rightly centres trans people's own testimonies, but also sensitively addresses the difficulties faced by partners, parents and siblings of people who transition, who may grieve for the person they thought they had known, and experience insecurity, anger and resentment. It recognises that while some trans people feel deeply hurt when their churches cannot offer liturgies for transition, or mark other life events such as reaffirming their relationships, others prefer not to undergo any ceremonies of this kind, and that a one-size-fits-all response is likely to be unsatisfactory. It also acknowledges the discomfort experienced by some church members when someone in the congregation transitions.

With their characteristic good humour and unswerving commitment to love and justice, Christina and Chris reassure readers that even small, simple steps are beneficial, and that congregations need not take an all-or-nothing approach: 'Do not try everything at once. Do the things that make the most difference to being fair... Take little steps to show the roof doesn't fall in when there is change.'

Dr Susannah Cornwall
Senior Lecturer in Constructive Theologies, University of Exeter
Director, Exeter Centre for Ethics and Practical Theology (EXCEPT)

Acknowledgements

We wish to thank especially the following people and organisations:

Those who kindly read and commented on the text at the manuscript stage – Liz Connelly, David Farey, Shanon Ferguson, Pauline Fleck, Jo Inkpin, Mark Lloyd, Kate Nicholas, Ann Reddecliffe, Lois Stone, Jane Thompson and Jack Woodruff.

The Sibyls, who kindly invited us to present some of the initial findings in this book at their weekend gathering in Thirsk in the summer of 2018.

Those who participated in our workshop sessions at day conferences held in September 2018 – OneBodyOneFaith's *Extending the Table* which focused on trans, non-binary and intersex people, and the United Reformed Church's *Beacon* conference on gender variance – and at the Gathering Voices day conference held in Stoke-on-Trent in October 2018.

Performance Activist Peterson Toscano, for permission to reproduce his poem, *Grave Robbers* (Appendix D).

Dr Susannah Cornwall for kindly writing the Foreword to this Guide.

The Authors

Christina (Tina) Beardsley SMMS, is a Church of England priest and retired healthcare chaplain who assists in her local parish in West London. Educated at Sussex, Cambridge and Leeds universities, Tina speaks and writes about chaplaincy, spirituality, gender and Victorian religion, and is a Visiting Scholar at Sarum College. A member of the Sibyls, a Christian spirituality group for transgender people, Tina has advocated for trans inclusion in the Church through a number of organisations and is due to chaplain the Modern Church Annual Conference in July 2020 which will focus on identity, sexuality and gender.

Chris Dowd was originally a minister in the LGBT-identified Metropolitan Community Churches for over a decade, planting a queer-friendly fresh expression called Journey in the West Midlands. At the same time, he served as a special category minister for the United Reformed Church as a University Chaplain at Aston University. Chris retrained as a minister of Word and Sacrament within the United Reformed Church and currently serves several churches. Chris is also an Honorary Research Fellow of Queen's College, Birmingham.

Introduction

We're so glad that you have picked up this book and hope that you will read it. What you find in its pages is important because it is about the lives, loves and humanity of other people. We invite you to approach what we have to say with respect, and without too much prejudgement. Our subject is how to ensure that your church or fellowship is inclusive of trans people.

This book is aimed primarily at the leadership, both lay and clergy, of any local church. It is difficult to cover every 'base' as church culture varies from tradition to tradition, location to location. We have written from an inclusive Catholic Anglican outlook and a 'middle of the road' United Reformed Church perspective, as these are our experience. We have attempted to consider both Catholic and more conservative viewpoints where possible. The book does assume a small amount of prior knowledge and is not designed to be a 'trans 101' book but rather a discussion of how to include trans people in your church.

Its second readership is all those interested in including people in your church. This may simply be that you are interested as a point of justice or you have been impacted by the gender journey of a friend or loved one. We've tried to keep things general enough that the book is of value to you as well.

This is our third collaborative writing project about trans people and the Church. Chris was a contributor to *This Is My Body: Hearing the Theology of Transgender People* (2016) which Tina co-edited with Michelle O'Brien. In 2018 we co-authored *Transfaith: A Transgender Pastoral Resource*, based on Chris's doctoral research into the spirituality of twelve transgender Christians. Rather than merely rephrasing what we have written before we have tried to cover new ground. For example, we have not included a glossary of trans terminology in this book because it already exists within *Transfaith*. While we briefly touch on

Natural Law, a whole chapter of *Transfaith* is dedicated to that. We will signpost this earlier work as you progress through the book.

We are both ordained ministers, Tina in the Church of England and Chris in the United Reformed Church, with decades of experience of pastoral ministry between us. We are both practical theologians committed to evidence-based methods – including interviews and narratives and engagement with the medical/therapeutic consensus – in dialogue with theology, especially the insights and practical wisdom of Scripture and the Christian tradition. Tina transitioned in 2001 and has been both advocate and activist for the full inclusion of trans people in the Church. Chris approached his doctoral research into trans people's spiritual journeys as a minister wanting to know more about how best to support trans people, and he has gone on learning.

Ideally, you will have already taken appropriate steps to include gender-variant people in your church and are reading this book to check that you are on the right lines. On the other hand, you may feel that you are only at the starting line as far as welcoming and affirming trans people is concerned. Or perhaps you consider yourself somewhere in between these two positions. Whatever your starting point, we believe that this book will be able to provide you with insights, guidance and resources on how to include trans people in your community. Our confidence lies in our evidence-based approach.

We have spent time listening to trans people and their loved ones to ensure that what is written here is grounded in their perceptions, needs and ideas of what you can do to make your church trans-friendly. We explain our methods later in this Introduction. The changes envisaged are not that radical. Indeed, what we suggest in this book will benefit your church and make it more inclusive for everyone.

One of the barriers to understanding trans people is that their differences – 'our' differences in Tina's case, so we'll use the first-person plural in this paragraph – are so often emphasised, rather than the humanity and faith we share with other Christians. We are rendered 'other' by medical language, by the media, and sometimes, sadly, by unhelpful 'church teaching'. Our lives are often exoticised, eroticised and stigmatised. Some of us 'blend in'; others do not, and 'standing out' can be dangerous. As a community we experience a high degree of social exclusion and minority stress – the chronic stress levels stigmatised minority groups can experience, due to interpersonal prejudice and discrimination, or poor social support and low socioeconomic status. We can be on the receiving end of violence and verbal, non-verbal and emotional abuse. The press is often intrusive and keen to tell our stories as they see them, rather than in our words and from our perspective. The reality of our experience and our very identity is questioned, publicly debated and even rubbished.

That's a long, and by no means comprehensive, list of negatives. Negativity and controversy on that scale might be making you nervous and wondering whether you really want to enter the fray. Please stick with us though. This book is designed to guide you through the maze of misinformation and hyperbole. It is an opportunity to learn. In any case, the Church is meant to be, and often is, a place of love, for trans people, as for everyone else, and what we outline should build on and be congruent with what you are already doing.

A vicar's story

Back in 2000 the Gender Trust, at that time the largest UK charity serving transgender people, approached Tina to write some pastoral guidelines about trans people aimed at clergy and congregations. The Trust's invitation came in response to a request for guidance of this kind from a vicar who had got to know a parishioner 'simply as a man with problems'. As the pastoral relationship developed, the man explained that he had transitioned, and that he was 'seeking reassurance that God accepts him'. An evangelical minister, the vicar described this encounter as:

> something of a revelation... Hearing his story has moved me...some approaches by certain Christian organisations [have] been decidedly unhelpful, judgemental and even cruel. The person needs support and help to enable them to be the person God has made them...this chap has achieved a stability because I have shown him that God loves him as he is. It is no longer an issue for him and he is simply getting on with his life. I am enormously indebted to him for what he has taught me.

Religious professionals are often expected to 'have all the answers' and to pretend that they do even when they don't! Pastoral and spiritual care based on ignorance is likely to be harmful and is potentially dangerous. Ministerial training can't cover every pastoral scenario and the needs of transgender people are unlikely to have been addressed. Including trans people's care in the curricula for ministerial formation would greatly help to increase awareness, deepen knowledge and improve trans people's experience of church life (see a suggested syllabus in Appendix A).

As the vicar noted, based only on a theology often rooted in the Genesis creation narratives, but without exploring the experience of trans Christians and their loved ones, some church leaders or bodies adopt the default position 'this is wrong', or fall back on theologies such as Natural Law. The impact on the trans person is usually violent and potentially abusive, verbally and emotionally. Faced with a reality that he did not previously know, this minister was open to listening and learning from the trans person and to having a dialogue with him. The outcome was extraordinary. The encounter was nothing short of a 'revelation'. The vicar was able to recognise God at work in this trans man's life and to reassure him of God's love for him. There was mutuality to this encounter: the minister both receiving God's grace from the trans man in front of him and ministering that grace to him in return.

Learning points from a vicar's story

- Some Christian approaches to trans people are harmful – we'll say more about them in later chapters – and should be avoided.

- Listening to a trans person – or their loved one – telling their story can be very moving and lead to new learning and even, in some cases, 'a revelation'.

- Being trans is not ungodly – again we'll say much more about this later in the book. At this stage it is enough just to note that your role is to reassure the person that they are loved by God as they are (just as we would reassure someone who is not trans).

Methodology

We have employed several methods that are well-established in practical theology. A brief outline of each method follows here.

The pastoral cycle

The pastoral cycle is often traced back to Roman Catholic social action movements in the early 20th century. It has been a key method in practical theology and an important tool within Latin American Liberation Theology (see below and Chapter 5) but is relevant wherever injustice or exclusion need to be addressed.

A typical cycle involves several stages, for example Ballard and Pritchard's (2006, first published 1996, pp.85–86) four stage model: Experience – Exploration – Reflection – Action (see Figure 1.1 below).

What all models have in common is that human experience (including the social context) will be taken seriously in the process. Practical theology, alert to power dynamics and the constant risk of injustice, tends to start from human experience, and only then begins to explore what is happening, drawing on the social sciences in dialogue with Christian sources.

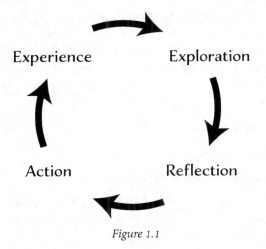

Experience   Exploration

Action   Reflection

Figure 1.1

Several theological methods are available at the reflective stage. In our work we are drawn to praxis models that combine lived experience with theory and narrative approaches, which are usually people's stories in their own words. We then make links with the fundamental Christian story. This intense engagement with a situation, and its significance, needs to lead to action and the kind of change that will improve people's lives.

This informed shift from experience, via learning, theory and reflection, to action is highly suited to a book of this kind, where the anticipated outcome is that you will want to change some things about your church life to make it more hospitable to trans people. Nor are such actions the final step, for the pastoral cycle is a spiral which means that current good practice will need to be examined, reviewed and improved on. We gladly invite you to use these kinds of tools to improve on the good practice we are advocating in this book.

Liberation Theology

The overriding belief in Liberation Theology is that God prefers the poor and oppressed and that blessing comes from the margins rather than the centre of the Church. Liberation Theology believes our duty as Christians is to challenge oppression in all its forms. Liberation Theology started in the 1970s as a critique of the economic and social oppressions of the South American poor. In the past 50 years it has broadened to explore and critique the systems of oppression that exist within the Church and wider society. Holland and Henriot (1983, first published 1980, p.28) pose three questions about social class, which seem equally pertinent in relation to trans people, or any other social minority:

1. Who makes the decisions?

2. Who benefits from the decisions?

3. Who bears the cost of the decisions?

Liberation Theology means we first have to listen to those who are oppressed and then ask, 'Where is God in this experience?' and 'What is an appropriate Christian response?' To this end we conducted workshops and interviews and have used the information we gained from them to write this book.

Narrative theology

A notable phenomenon when Christians discuss trans people is the criticism of relying too heavily on trans people's stories, combined with the claim that the Church 'still needs to do the theology' about transgender people. We make no apology for grounding our approach here in trans people's stories and dispute the idea that trans people's stories and the Church's theology about them can be separated in this way.

Given that the Bible is largely a collection of stories, it's intriguing that the Church has a history of ignoring stories when it suits its purpose, as Don Cupitt (1995, first published 1991, p.42) has pointed out:

> At the drop of a hat theologians would reel off the old philosophical criticisms of pagan myths, images and sacrifices. Yet somehow they tacitly exempted their own narratives, images and rituals from the same criticism... It was all very odd. Philosophy condemned stories for stirring up our emotions and seducing us into identifying ourselves with the central characters. But if this is generally a bad thing, how does it suddenly become a good thing when the central character is St Ursula or Jesus?

Rowan Williams (1979, pp.2–3) explains how the Incarnation of God in human form in the person of Jesus Christ is the most powerful critique and counterbalance to this tendency:

> By affirming that all 'meaning', every assertion about the significance of life and reality, must be judged by reference to a brief succession of contingent events in Palestine, Christianity – almost without realizing it – closed off the path to 'timeless truth'... Even when Christian writers use language suggesting such a picture, there are strong forces pulling in an opposite direction, demanding the affirmation of history, and thus of human change and growth, as significant. If the heart of 'meaning' is a human story, a story of growth, conflict and death, every human story, with all its oddity and ambivalence, becomes open to interpretation in terms of God's saving work.

It is our conviction that all of us have much to learn, both spiritually and theologically from the stories of the Christian trans people and their loved ones that we interviewed for this book.

Group interviews

Interview participants were recruited via internet networks such as the Facebook group, *Christians for LGBTI+ Equality*. The times, dates and locations of the groups – held in London and the north of England in the spring of 2018 – were advertised on these forums and people were encouraged to come and participate. People self-selected to participate and were told very clearly that they could withdraw at any time.

Two different workshops were held on the same day in both locations. The first was a discussion group with trans people about how to make the Church more trans friendly which is reported in Chapter 6. The second group was the parents and partners who came with their loved one to take part in the second group, and these findings are reported in Chapter 4. We also quote our participants throughout the book.

The purpose of the interviews was explained, and permissions were received before the interview began. The interviews were recorded and transcribed, and the transcripts sent to the interviewees to correct or delete to ensure they adequately represented the thoughts and feelings of the participants. Names have been changed so that participants are not identifiable.

Introducing our interviewees

Anne is a trans woman in later middle age. Her faith background is Anglican. She is a campaigner and advocate for the inclusion of trans people within the Church and is active within many trans organisations and social groups.

Becky is the mother of **Angela** who is a young trans woman currently studying at university. Becky grew up in a very conservative Non-conformist church and has struggled to find places within her tradition where she and Angela have been welcomed and affirmed. She would still describe herself as more conservative than liberal theologically. She has several other children.

David is a young trans man who grew up within the Quaker tradition and who currently attends an LGBT-friendly Evangelical Church. He came out and transitioned some time ago. His mother **Sophie** was also part of the group.

Ed is a young man who was in the process of transitioning at the time of interview. He grew up in a churched family where his father was employed by the Church. He is in a relationship with **Rachel** and they both attend an LGBT-affirming church.

George comes from a Greek family and has an Orthodox Church background. He is currently not attending church regularly.

Jim is a young man who is currently studying at a university where he met his partner Steve. His background is Anglican, and since attending university his faith journey has begun in earnest.

Maria, who transitioned in middle age, converted from Anglicanism to Catholicism earlier in her life and currently attends Mass daily.

Rachel grew up in a conservative church which she has now left. She and **Ed** met at church before Ed began to transition.

Sophie is the mother of **David**. She is a Quaker and has another son as well as David.

Steve is studying at the same university as Jim and both are heavily involved in their city centre Anglican congregation.

We could not have written this book in its current form, without the generosity of those who participated in the workshops we held in the spring of 2018 and this book is dedicated to them.

It is also dedicated to the memory of a clergy pioneer of pastoral and spiritual care for trans people, Canon A.R. Millbourn, a Church of England priest, who in the 1940s supported Michael Dillon/Lobzang Jivaka (see his autobiography published in 2017) – a trans man and ship's doctor – and also wrote the Foreword to the autobiography of trans woman, Roberta Cowell (1954, p.3), which is part dedicated to him. Much is written about trans people being a very recent cultural phenomenon. This is not so, and nor is their care by Christian clergy. There is a fine tradition of Christian ministry to trans people, albeit much of it was relatively hidden in the past. We salute those who have gone before us with gratitude, and hope that this guidebook will assist you and countless others to promote the full inclusion of trans people, not just in your own congregation, but in the whole Church of God.

Chapter 1

Understanding Who Trans People Are

Introducing some Christian trans people

This book is not about 'an issue'; it's about people. To address the subject of this chapter – understanding who trans people are – we will consider some technical terms and the multi-disciplinary consensus about the care of trans and gender nonconforming people. It's vital to remember that the word 'trans' or 'transgender' is an *adjective* and has to be completed by a *noun* – 'people' or 'person', 'woman' or 'man'.

In social interactions, and especially in a pastoral book such as this, the focus should always be on people and their humanity. So, we want to begin by introducing you to some people, Abi, Jason, Robin, and Debbie (not their real names). They, or people like them, could be future members of your church, or might already be there in your congregation.

Meet Abi:

I'm Abi and I've been an Evangelical Christian since my late teens, so it took many years to realise that Deuteronomy 22.5 was not directed at trans people at all. My school, of which I'm proud to be an old boy/girl, was Evangelical in ethos. As an adult and a middle-class professional, I am also somewhere in the middle as far as my gender identity is concerned. Part of my life is lived as male, and part as female; I describe myself as bigender. That can be difficult for the people around me to accept, but it isn't difficult for me. I had to hide the female 'me' for far too long, but now I am free to live comfortably in both gender roles.

Being someone who has no desire to transition to female comes with its own problems. People sometimes say to me, 'We find your situation very confusing, but if you were to transition, it would be much easier to accept you.'

When I did 'come out' to my church the reaction from the vicar and many in the congregation was very condemning and they wrote letters to me and my wife to show the strength of their feelings. I'd had a leadership role in the church as a PCC (Parochial Church Council) member, singer/songwriter and worship leader, but all that came to an end following my disclosure. My wife and I had no alternative but to leave the church. It was the place where we had met, married, and served God for several decades. Our bishop was very helpful and pointed us to a more welcoming church. After we moved, we settled in well, but the vicar at that time was fairly cautious about the situation and I was not convinced that the warm welcome we had received extended to being able to attend services as Abi. People told me that they would find that very difficult. However, we now have a new vicar who is keen that Abi should be able to come to church, so I have started to do that on an occasional basis, with a variety of reactions. It's a work in progress, and the vicar shares our vision for a church inclusive of all diversities, not just trans people. And now this has developed into being able to use my music to lead worship in church as Abi – another step along the journey to full acceptance.

It's great that you've met Abi. She's inspirational: a gifted singer and musician, whose song is one of biblical inclusion. Listening to her we can see that relating to someone who is trans might involve relating to a spouse or loved one as well. This is something that came through very strongly in the workshops we held in preparing this book. Abi's story also illustrates something we've seen already: how important the clergy person or minister can be in determining whether the trans person will be rejected by, merely tolerated by or fully included in their church. David, one of our workshop participants, suggested some questions that they would like to ask a minister before joining their church:

Do you tolerate me, or do you want something...are you interested?

Is this something you've thought about before?

Is it something you're interested in thinking about?

Similarly, Becky, the parent of a trans daughter, explains:

> I don't want Angela to be tolerated in a church. I want her to be warmly welcomed and to become part of a family.

The rejection Abi and her wife experienced became a wound that proved difficult to heal. Their bishop behaved as a chief shepherd and guardian by directing them to a church where they were made more welcome. Even this was conditional though as only her male persona was welcome at church. Abi apparently had no place in the 'holy space' of church. This experience led her to think about other people who were being marginalised by the church community. She was able to share her vision for inclusion when a new vicar was appointed. This priest was also passionate about justice and acceptance and spent time engaging with Abi. It has made a huge difference in terms of Abi's sense of belonging to that church and she soon started to attend church services and events. More recently, Abi has been invited to lead the music in worship. She has even written her own song about inclusion. People who hear it are struck by the depth of the words and join in the celebration of unity.

Learning points from Abi's story

- *Trans*, short for *transgender*, is an umbrella term that covers a range of people not simply those who transition to and then live permanently in the gender that matches their gender identity.

- Trans people may carry wounds of rejection inflicted by family, friends and their faith community.

- They have gifts to offer that may have been denied expression in other Christian settings just because they have come out as trans.

- The trans person may be accompanied by their spouse or family who may also need your support: we'll be saying more about this in Chapter 4.

- A conditional welcome may seem better than rejection but is still conditional.

- If you are not informed about trans people, the arrival of someone trans in your congregation is an opportunity for the ministers and church community to learn and grow.

- The trans person may be able to help the church community gain a fuller vision of what an inclusive church might look like.

Meet Jason:

Hi, I'm Jason. I've always been willing to talk about myself to other Christians, in the hope that they'd gain a better understanding of what it's like to be trans, though, to be honest, I'm less inclined to explain myself these days. Hormones and top surgery have changed my body and I prefer to get on with life as a man rather than always being the token trans person. I'm not in total stealth [meaning, fully assimilated as one's gender and not inclined to declare that one has transitioned], and will sometimes 'out' myself to discuss my journey, especially with fellow Christians, as some seem to be so prejudiced against us. That's why I'm happy for Tina and Chris to quote me in their book. I've had a Christian upbringing, and my parents are very involved in church life, so I know it inside out and believe I have a calling to ministry. Although I was brought up as a girl, I've always been very self-aware: I was the proverbial tomboy and confident that transition was the right step for me. Thankfully my parents have been fully supportive. As a student, my life was pretty full with study and worship, and being trans hasn't been such a big deal to me as it might be for older trans people. Discernment for ministry became interesting when I was told that trans candidates need to have 'completed' transition before they can be recommended for training. In fact, this is not in the Church of England's official guidance about transgender candidates and turned out to be false. Presumably it was based on the mistaken equation of transition with surgery. I've noticed that non-trans people often seem to focus on trans people's surgeries as if that's what transition is mainly about.

For example, some Christian friends wondered – and even used to ask me – if I've 'mutilated' my body. Even though I'd shared my own self-understanding with them, comments like that suggested they hadn't grasped that my transition was actually about wholeness.

Jason resembles other people quoted in this book. All are prepared to tell their stories so that others can gain insight into their experience. Maybe there's a 'Jason' in your congregation. Someone who transitioned in the past and is happily living out their gender identity. No one else is going to know unless they choose to tell them.

As Jason explained, having a trans history is no longer an issue for him. His loving Christian upbringing gave him the stability to accept himself. Which is just as well, because some Christian friends have tended to say things or ask questions that would probably make them flinch if put to them. Questioning can promote understanding, and no one wants to shut down dialogue, but the language we use – e.g. 'mutilation' – could be hurtful for the trans person. Helping one another to be and become the person God has made us should be our aim.

Jason's stability helped him to come to terms with these kinds of comments, but when he tried to enter the discernment process for ministry it appeared that trans people were perceived as a problem, especially during transition. Guidance grounded in evidence and good practice is the ideal. The requirement that Jason encountered, which was not official policy, appeared to assume that transition was inherently destabilising, rather than increasing the trans person's wellbeing. The church official concerned appeared to lack insight into trans people's experience.

Learning points from Jason's story

- Some people with a transgender history may not want to talk about their past and you may be unaware of it unless they tell you.

- With more information and role models than in the past, younger trans people may find it easier to come out and address their gender identity (though see Debbie's story below and the section on role models in Chapter 6).

- Even so, not everyone has a stable home and unconditional parental love, so you may need to give support and reassurance.

- Think carefully about the words you will use and ensure that they are sensitively expressed: avoid questions that would make you feel uncomfortable if asked of you.

> • Trans people in the Church often encounter institutional barriers. Making the Church inclusive of trans people means working to remove them.

Meet Robin:

My name is Robin and always has been. It's just the spelling that's changed. When I was young it was spelt with a 'y' – Robyn, and I was brought up as a girl, but I was glad to have a name that, when spoken, could be masculine or feminine, because that's how, increasingly, I've come to understand myself: as both male and female.

The terms I use about myself are genderqueer or non-binary. Being given the name Robyn was very convenient as I've only had to change one letter to express who I am today! I prefer the masculine version of the name nowadays but am equally at ease with behaviours our society tends to regard as feminine. I'm happy to bring out childhood photographs in which my hair is long and I'm wearing a floaty dress, even though today my hair is cropped short and I always wear trousers, and at work, a man's business suit. In meetings it can startle people when I speak. They're surprised that this masculine looking person has such a high-pitched feminine voice, and I have no plans to change that; or again, when I take my knitting needles from my briefcase and start knitting to aid my concentration during a tricky item on the agenda. Maybe my appearance, voice pitch and intonation and knitting are stereotypical, but these are some of the ways gender is constructed in our society. My experience is that I'm very happy exploring the wide range of options that are open to both men and women. I'd feel limited and constrained were I to have to opt for one rather than the other. Over the years I've become far more masculine in my appearance without having to shed certain aspects of my femininity. None of this has been a problem in my church, which is progressive and fully inclusive of trans people, as it is of lesbian, gay and bisexual people. In recent years my ministry has been mainly with asylum seekers in the UK, but I've also worked to support trans and gender nonconforming people in other churches which are not as inclusive as the one I belong to.

Here Robin helps us to appreciate that not everyone sees gender as a male or female option. For some trans people transition is about expressing a gender identity that has been at odds with their assigned gender. By contrast, *genderqueer* or *non-binary* people like Robin have a sense of themselves as being both masculine and feminine; as neither; or 'beyond' a female or male binary in some way. It's important to note as well that being non-binary is about *gender identity* and not *gender expression*. In other words, a non-binary person may well present in a conventionally masculine or feminine way. It's their internal sense of gender that does not tick the conventional male or female boxes.

More people, especially young people, are finding it easier to identify as non-binary. This is mainly due to increased social acceptance. Non-binary people have always existed. In the past, unless one had social privilege and could defy social conventions, people were more likely to hide the fact that they were non-binary.

Many traditional cultures today envisage and sanction third (male living as a female) or fourth (female living as a male) and sometimes other gender options, as have ancient cultures in the past (see below). Where gender is regarded as a spectrum, or as fluid, there are more options for people and an opportunity to explore gender roles which other societies might forbid or place off limits. Gender theory has examined numerous so-called 'masculine' and 'feminine' behaviours or qualities, noting the artificiality of these associations, and how such stereotyping can limit options for everyone. According to theorist Judith Butler (2006, first published 1990, pp.xxxiii–xxxiv), these stereotypical masculine and feminine behaviours are socially constructed rather than 'natural', but derive their power and influence from largely unconscious processes of repetition that begin in childhood and that she describes as gender's 'performativity'.

Robin has benefitted from changes in UK culture that have promoted the equality of men and women. It remains a work in progress, and because patriarchy – literally the 'rule of the fathers' or male privilege – remains strong, it is still easier for someone born female bodied, like Robin, to adopt and blend masculine traits and appearance, than for someone born male to adopt and blend feminine ones. Breaking down gender stereotypes does not make someone trans. *Gender nonconformity* is principally about behaviour rather than identity. For example, a woman who thinks and behaves in stereotypically masculine ways may be challenging gender expectations within her culture but still retain a strong sense of identity as a woman. For others though, like Robin, gender nonconformity can be a way of expressing a non-binary gender identity.

This is where the media has often caused confusion about transgender children. For children to play and dress at variance with stereotypes associated with their assigned birth gender does not mean that they're about to be rushed towards hormone blockers and early transition. (In the UK cross-gender hormone therapy and surgery cannot be accessed by someone under 16 years old.) These behaviours have to be accompanied by the child's insistence that their gender differs from their birth assigned gender (NHS 2008, p.17). Only a small number of gender nonconforming children grow up to identify as trans. The care of children who identify as non-binary is also a specialist area and clinics are increasingly attuned to their needs.

Learning points from Robin's story

- It's inevitable that we look at gender through our own experience and mainstream culture.

- The way our culture understands *biological sex* (bodies) and *gender* (social expression) has changed significantly over the past century.

- There is a tendency to revert to older social patterns of gender when someone appears to challenge current gender norms: we need to be aware of this and avoid it.

- Gender inequalities affect transgender people as they do others.

- Gender nonconforming children can be very vulnerable, largely due to the anxiety of others.

- Churches can model acceptance and care of those who are different, including those who are gender nonconforming, or who express a genderqueer or non-binary identity.

- 'Traditional' churches can model this inclusive ethos as much as 'progressive' churches, though that can be a struggle, as the next story shows.

Meet Debbie:

Hello! My name is Debbie, short for Deborah, and I deliberately chose a biblical name because my Christian faith has always been important to me. I was raised by devout Christian parents and growing up it seemed that everyone in my family circle – aunts and uncles, grandparents and cousins – were Christians. I suppose you'd describe their attitudes as conservative, but they were always loving so I wasn't prepared for the conflict and hurt my transition was going to cause for those around me. It felt like World War III at the time!

I grew up knowing that I was 'different' but didn't seem to be able to find a 'name' for what I was experiencing. I heard the occasional negative sermon about gay people. I was attracted mainly to boys, so I assumed that I was gay, and knew that I was going to have to hide the fact; which I did, for a while. I'm so blessed with my parents. Their love really is unconditional, and as I entered my late teens I decided to tell them. They were not totally surprised, but it still came as a shock. They said they'd always love me, no matter what, but they were fearful for the future and warned me that some members of our family were likely to find my news a challenge.

I can't tell you what a relief it was to 'come out' to my parents and then to my closest friends. It meant that I could talk and talk and begin to express myself more fully, but the more I did that, and started to learn about the range of people who are 'different', I began to realise that the label 'gay' didn't really fit my experience. Yes, I was attracted to boys, but being free to say so seemed to release the barrier that had prevented me from saying that I was a girl – Debbie. I began to tell a small handful of trusted friends, who were very supportive, but how would my parents cope?

When I told them they were terribly shocked. They'd only just begun to get used to the fact that I was gay which, as they predicted, had not gone down well with some of our relatives and at our church. My parents knew even less about trans people at that point, but what they did know made them very anxious about the reaction of family members, and our church, and their fears were totally justified. As far as our church was concerned I was an abomination and my parents were told in no uncertain terms not to support me, indeed to disown me, were I to transition. Bless them, they have stood by me, but the price has been a huge rift in our family, and eventually my parents were presented with an ultimatum, which meant that they had to leave that church, a church community they'd loved and served for many years.

I'm so grateful to my parents for standing by me but can't help feeling guilty for what I've put them through. They've worked so hard to find out about trans people, including the science behind gender variance, and have discovered how their instinct to support me in my transition, as their beloved child, is actually borne out by the specialists in this area. It took tremendous strength and courage on their part to resist, when people they respected, including church leaders, were telling them they should do all they could to prevent me from transitioning. I guess the first coming out had already confirmed that I was a much happier person, and while they continue to be concerned for me, as someone who is trans, they could see that I 'knew my own mind'. I can't thank them enough for that and am so proud to be their daughter.

Debbie's coming out story raises several important topics: the difference between sexual orientation and gender identity; the role of family dynamics; the impact of church culture; the benefits of being well-informed about how gender variance arises and is managed.

Modern communication, especially the internet, has made it easier for young people to come out as trans early on in their lives. Information is more accessible and role models are more visible. This is confirmed by Maria, who grew up in an earlier era, and observes: 'I didn't have an understanding of who or what I was.'

Not so very long ago, societal expectations around gender were so rigid and the stigma attached to being transgender so great, that some people hid who they were from their families and partners. Many have only come out in recent decades as attitudes have become more accepting. Some trans people in the 1960s and early 1970s came out as gay or lesbian and only later came out as trans. This was partly because at that time 'gay' and 'lesbian', although primarily signifying sexual orientation, acted partly as generic terms covering a range of identities, including variant gender identity (Brooker 2017). Being gay and lesbian then was not necessarily easy, but easier for some than admitting that one was gender-variant and might wish to consider transition.

Debbie's two-stage coming out, as gay and then trans, a pattern I (Chris) observed among middle-aged trans people in my earlier interviews (Dowd and Beardsley 2018), can still occur today. Debbie's social life appears to have been sheltered by the conservative church culture inhabited by her family. She'd heard of gay people, but only when she had come out as gay herself discovered that there were trans people as well. It was then she found her true community.

Ed, a young trans male, also recorded a dual coming out:

> I came out around sexuality first a few years ago... And then last year I came out around gender.

Some people mistakenly assume that gay people and trans people are the same and Debbie's story might appear to confirm that, but it's not so. Trans people can be straight (attracted to someone of the opposite gender to their gender identity), gay (attracted to someone of the same gender as their gender identity), bisexual (attracted to someone of any gender or sex) or asexual (without, or with minimal, sexual attraction to someone of any gender or sex). Gender identity is different from sexual orientation and trans people's journeys may make their sexual orientation difficult to classify. For example, someone who is apparently in a lesbian relationship and then transitions as male may appear to be in a heterosexual relationship, but how a couple understands their relationship is for them and not for other people to say. How a trans person identifies in terms of sexual orientation is up to them and shouldn't be assumed.

Learning points from Debbie's story

- There is more in the media about trans people and greater general knowledge about gender variance, but it doesn't follow that it's always easier for young people to come out as trans than it was in the past.

- Being trans refers to one's *gender identity* and is different from *sexual orientation*, which refers to the gender of the person one is attracted to, or that one is asexual (someone without sexual feelings or desires or whose attractions don't require sexual expression).

- Equality legislation protects trans people in the public social sphere, but among family and friends, hurtful things can be said about them, or to them.

- When families are divided over a family member's transition, their minister and congregation may have a healing, reconciling role to play.

- It can be especially difficult to come out as trans in conservative Christian circles.

- Some theologies prejudge the trans person rather than engaging with their experience of gender and of God – we will explore a more inclusive theological approach in Chapter 3.

Many of the problems Debbie and her family experienced were because her church was so ill-informed about trans people. This is why we commend good pastoral practice based on a practical theology model that takes account of both experience and knowledge as well as Christian faith. The remainder of this chapter considers two important topics. First, trans people's experience of being trans. Second, some basic knowledge of trans people, including terminology and what specialists say about their care.

Transgender people's experience of being trans – what some of our participants said

Each one of us has a gender identity. For those who are *cisgender*, i.e., people who are not trans, (*cis* being the Latin for 'on the same side') their gender identity matches their gender as assigned at birth based on their biological sex. Trans people, on the other hand, experience a mismatch or disjunction between their gender as assigned at birth (usually based on their genitals or their secondary sex characteristics) and their gender identity.

For example, parents and family may be raising a child as a girl on the presumption that she will develop into woman, but the child identifies as a boy and will at some stage transition and live as a man. We're not referring to girls who behave as 'tomboys': playing with boys, preferring their games and sports and adopting a stereotypical 'boyish' appearance. Such a child could grow up to be trans, but there is more to the trans experience than that. Either as child, adolescent or adult (or at all three stages) the trans individual will experience strong identification with the gender to which they eventually transition; or, if they are *non-binary* or *genderqueer*, they do not identify with being male nor female.

Most people who are not trans take their own gender identity for granted. The difference for trans people is they experience a discrepancy between who they are and who other people presume them to be. This leads them to think a great deal about their gender identity, as Steve observes:

> I had to think about it a lot and rethink who I truly am before I managed to come to any kind of conclusion.

For some people, coming to terms with being trans can be a difficult path. The experience often begins quite early in life, but as Maria explains, it can be quashed by social pressure:

> I was quite a religious child I had quite a strong faith in God... But also an intense desire to be a girl and not a boy... But I think I rapidly learned that was not allowed and... Repressed it and denied it and tried to live as a boy... And then as a man...

She also discovered that religious prejudice against trans people can be internalised:

> Well I was struggling with a lot of guilt issues in life... I had not come to terms with myself in any way... Whatever it was it was unholy and ungodly and wrong and sinful...

Trans people can go to considerable lengths to deny who they are, including hyper-masculine or hyper-feminine behaviours or careers (Brown 2006). In the past, and maybe still today, people have married someone of the seemingly opposite sex to 'prove' their birth assigned gender to themselves and others. It rarely (if ever) works, with the resulting fall out for loved ones, especially if their spouse had no idea that they were trans. Maria again:

> I got married... You know again totally repressing my gender identity
> and committing myself to the marriage... [it] became a very unhappy
> marriage... I had two daughters... Finally, my gender issues became
> too powerful and my marriage failed, and the family collapsed in ruins.

Steve, who is much younger than Maria, and transitioned before going
to university, realises that he has been 'very fortunate' in terms of
acceptance. At a church barbeque, a girl outed him as being trans to
an adult:

> I looked like I do now... But I was under a different name... And the
> adults knew me as a girl and this kid said to one of the adults, 'Look
> that is a boy who is actually a girl.' And she was like, 'No you're having
> me on.' And it was like 'That is not a boy right there.' And I was like, 'No
> it's true I am a guy in a girl's body' and she was just really surprised
> and really accepting... She has a nursing background and it was nice
> to hear that not just from a Christian but also someone who is in the
> medical profession.

Healthcare employees are familiar with and subject to the provisions of
the Equality Act 2010, which protects trans people from discrimination,
so one would expect a nurse to be respectful and supportive. The
Equality Act refers to trans people as those intending to, undergoing
or having undergone *gender reassignment*, which sounds narrowly
clinical. The legislation, though, also covers those who have undergone
a *social transition* rather than a *medical transition* and indeed anyone,
including those who are non-binary, genderqueer, bigender, and those
who cross-dress only occasionally, who identify as transgender. It
would also probably cover gender nonconforming people who are not
trans on the assumption that they are.

Steve's final sentence is a reminder that religion and medicine, with
other cultural forces, have both shaped the language about trans people,
and the attitudes to them, for good and ill.

Trans people – the evolving history of terminology and clinical care

The terms and language about trans people can seem somewhat
bewildering. To the beginner they may even be a source of anxiety:

will one say the wrong thing and insult someone? (Sometimes you might be unsure whether the person is trans, and wonder whether to ask will offend them, whether or not they are trans. In that case it's safer not to ask.) The best policy is to allow the trans person you are talking with to lead the conversation. If they've not already mentioned it (and you think it appropriate) ask them to tell you the terms and *pronouns* they would prefer you to use. Remember, though, that some people may not actually want you to draw attention to the fact that they are trans.

In meetings that are intentionally inclusive of gender-variant people it has become the custom to ask everyone present to declare their preferred pronouns. This is an example of good practice. Asked what would make them feel comfortable at church, Ed said:

> I guess it would come from interacting with people... I guess them being receptive to using my correct pronouns... Or at least making an effort to... Kind of being on board with that is a good way of like showing me... Acknowledging me... Yeah... That's an immediate sign I guess.

The reason there are so many terms is because trans people have a long history and have existed in many different cultures. Mollenkott (2001) cites examples from the ancient Near Eastern world, including ancient Egypt, as well as contemporary examples. For example, *acault* 'males' in Myanmar Buddhism are believed to have been chosen by a female spirit, and like the *Hijras* in India and Pakistan, perform a sacred alternative gender role. 'Two-Spirit people' among Native American tribes and society are another well-known example.

Part 1 of *Trans Britain* (Burns 2018) includes stories of trans people who were around in the mid-20th century and earlier, some of whom found it necessary to hide the fact they were trans. In those days, the most widely available term was '*sex change*' which was common in tabloid newspaper narratives. This sensationalised trans people's lives. It is no longer an acceptable term because transition involves 'confirming' one's gender identity and *not* altering it. It is the trans person's *gender expression, gender presentation* or *gender role* that changes. The intention is to claim the gender identity that they have always had but may have supressed to that point, rather than acquiring a different gender.

Like most human groups trans people are also quite diverse and one term is not enough. We tend to use the neat catch-all, *trans* as a term to include all gender nonconforming identities but there are different communities under the *trans* umbrella. In the modern West, trans people's care has been supervised by the medical profession for well over a century. Doctors love to coin clinical terms with a Greek or Latin etymology.

Transsexual is a good example. It is a combination of two Latin words: 'trans' meaning crossing over, and 'sexual' which refers not to the libido, but to the sexed body as being either male or female. Some trans people still use this term, but it belongs to an earlier clinical era and is less common today. There are several reasons why it's dropped out of use.

First, during the past half century we have gone through a social and linguistic revolution which has led to differences between male and female being discussed in terms of *gender* rather than *sex*. As a result, we use the term *transgender*. Trans people are often happier with the term 'transgender' which clearly indicates that their concern is with their gender identity, not their sexuality.

Second, the older term 'transsexual' tends to be associated with the idea that someone who *transitions* is 'crossing over' from one gender to another. But as we have explained, someone who transitions is not changing their gender, (though they could be said, should they undergo a medical transition, to have changed their sex). They are taking steps to be recognised by those around them as the gender they have identified with for the whole of their lives. This is why we prefer the term *gender confirmation surgery* rather than *gender reassignment surgery*.

Despite common assumptions to the contrary, not all surgeries are genital. For many trans men, 'top surgery', or double mastectomy, is an essential step, as facial feminisation surgery can be for some trans women. For many trans people these are more important than genital surgery, as they help them to navigate the world with more confidence in their gender presentation.

Third, 'transsexual' like the more recent term *gender dysphoria* (which refers to the discomfort or distress trans people can experience until they transition) is a clinical term, and trans people are beginning to set aside this medical model of 'diagnosis' and 'treatment' and articulate their experience for themselves. A consultation to reform the UK's Gender Recognition Act 2004 was held in the autumn of 2018.

Its premise was that the gender recognition process should be less medicalised, without the need for a 'diagnosis' of gender dysphoria or the submission of clinical notes. Trans people don't necessarily feel dysphoric about their gender variance, nor do they always see a clinician; some simply transition with or without hormones, though hormone therapy should always entail medical supervision.

Modern medicine has played a crucial role in the care of trans people, enabling them to transition in ways earlier generations of gender-variant people could only dream of. This has enabled people to appreciate that gender and sexual orientation are two different aspects of human experience. I (Tina) can remember, back in the 1960s, a boy from my school being arrested for *cross-dressing* (wearing the clothes of the opposite sex), and who in retrospect was presumably trans, but the main charge was for soliciting sex with men. There was a confusion of sexuality and gender identity then that would be less likely to happen today.

Gender identity clinics, which began to open from the 1960s (the oldest, founded in 1966, and probably the most well-known, is the clinic originally based at Charing Cross[1]) helped trans people to escape criminalisation and turned them into patients. This was not all gain, as being a patient could mean loss of autonomy and trans people were made to jump through unreasonable clinical hoops to receive treatment. Prior to this date these treatments had only been available to those who could afford them. It would take decades for trans people to be seen as clients and stakeholders with regard to their treatment, due to the stigma attached to being gender-variant.

In the early days of sexology (the science of sexual orientation and gender variance), in the late 19th and early 20th century, anything other than cisgender heterosexuality was considered deviant. Gender variance was often seen as a subset of homosexuality and was treated (in some jurisdictions) as a mental illness that could be 'cured' by talking therapies or by invasive treatments like electro-convulsive therapy. Geoff Brown's 1966 novel *I Want What I Want* is a transition narrative that I (Tina) read aged 15 when it was first published. It begins in a mental hospital where the protagonist (introduced with a male name) has been committed for cross-dressing. Once discharged,

---

1   Now based in West London and part of the Tavistock and Portman NHS Foundation Trust.

they transition as Wendy, but accessing treatment proves difficult. Medical transition was not then generally available, though this was just about to change.

Magnus Hirschfeld (1991, first published 1910) was a famous sexologist who worked with gender-variant people at the beginning of the 20th century. He concluded that trans people were a discrete group and pioneered humane methods of treatment that included gender confirmation surgery. In the mid-century Harry Benjamin, an endocrinologist, developed *hormone therapy* as a breakthrough treatment option and which continues today as part of people's medical transition.

Neither of these clinicians regarded gender-variant people as deviant or mentally ill, but other sections of the medical establishment took longer to catch up. The *Diagnostic and Statistical Manual for Mental Diseases* continued to include the category of 'gender identity disorder' until 2013, when it was replaced by that of 'gender dysphoria', a term more acceptable to trans stakeholders. In 2018 the World Health Organization removed what it calls *'gender incongruence'* from the mental health chapter in the *International Classification of Diseases – 11* after consulting trans people and a rigorous review of the evidence. In both instances, being trans was declassified as a mental health problem. This is long after homosexuality was declassified in 1973. It is frequently observed that trans people often lag behind lesbian and gay people in terms of equality.

The same kind of debates that led to the conclusion that being gay or lesbian is a natural human variation are being repeated about trans people in our society at the moment. The media highlights trans celebrities, but trans people's lives are constantly contested – for example, the slogan, 'trans women aren't real women' adopted by some radical feminists (see Chapter 3).

Trans people are also more vulnerable to fragile mental health due to discrimination. The UK Government's *National LGBT Survey Research Report* (HM Government 2018) noted that 40 per cent of trans respondents had experienced a negative reaction on accessing health services because of their gender identity, compared to 13 per cent of cisgender respondents, who were treated negatively because of their sexual orientation. Similarly, the *Stonewall School Report* (2017) shows that more than four in five (84%) of trans pupils have self-harmed, compared to three in five (61%) lesbian, gay or bi young people. More than two in five (45%) of trans pupils have attempted suicide, compared to one in five (22%) of cisgender pupils. In one of the workshops we held, the families of two young trans people told us that one had overdosed and another came close to it.

These mental health problems are usually related to the social stigma still attached to being trans and are not integral to being transgender. It is true that in the 1980s, consultant psychiatrists became the principal gatekeepers for trans people's treatment, but this was mainly to ensure that the person had sufficient mental stability to transition. Today, the care of trans people tends to be multi-disciplinary in character.

The World Professional Association for Transgender Health (WPATH) is the leading international multi-disciplinary body in the field and its evidenced-based Standards of Care (SOC) Version 7 are emphatic that:

- Being transgender is a human variation and not a pathology.

- It is both ineffective and unethical to attempt to persuade someone to alter their gender identity – (i.e. being trans is not a 'choice').

WPATH emerged in the late 1970s and was originally named after the esteemed clinician of transgender care, Harry Benjamin. It aimed to promote humane, evidence-based treatment following the withdrawal of gender confirmation surgery by the gender identity service at Johns Hopkins University in the US. The withdrawal of confirmation surgery was at the instigation of Dr Paul McHugh, a conservative Catholic. McHugh continues to expound views that are contrary to what developed into the WPATH principles. He regards being trans as a mental illness and believes that trans people's minds should be altered to prevent them from transitioning. His writings are seized on by conservatives, including conservative Christians, who often quote his belief that being trans is a mental illness to support their theological conviction that trans people's behaviours can and should be restrained.

We return to this topic in Chapter 3 (where we look at the impact of the culture wars on trans people) but as a rule of thumb: talks or books that refer to trans people's 'gender confusion' and emphasise their 'gender dysphoria' usually assume that trans people have a psychological 'problem' that can be 'cured'. This is in defiance of the UK's therapeutic consensus condemning conversion therapy and calls from Church and State for it to be banned.

The *Memorandum of Understanding on Conversion Therapy, Version 2*, of October 2017 was signed by many UK therapeutic bodies, including the Royal College of General Practitioners, the British Psychological Society and the British Association for Counselling and Psychotherapy. Version 1 aimed to protect the public from efforts to change a person's sexual orientation. Version 2 extends this aim to gender identity.

There is a scientific basis to this therapeutic consensus. The significant study by Zhou and colleagues (1995) appears to be supported by subsequent research as summarised by Roughgarden 2017 (pp.50–2), who reports that 'many studies are now reporting that the physical brain structure of transgender people more closely resembles the sex they identify with rather than with their genital sex.' This evidence confirms that trans people are not confused cisgender people, sexual deviants or mentally ill. They are simply different from cisgender people and no less worthy of respect.

Chapter 2

What the Bible Really Tells Us About Trans People

Introduction

This chapter looks at several ideas simultaneously. It begins with a discussion of how the Bible is read. We have come to believe that this is the core of 'the controversy' regarding trans people and the many other sharp disagreements that exist about gender and sexuality within the Church.

The chapter also considers several theological tools that will help create a trans-friendly theology. First, we look at biblical characters who may provide inspiration to those seeking to find gender-variant people within the pages of the Bible. We then briefly summarise our chapter on Natural Law from *Transfaith* before exploring one of the controversies of the early Church, and what it can tell us about our arguments about inclusion today. Finally, we discuss principles that should guide any discussion of gender-variant people (or any people for that matter) no matter how the Bible is read.

While there is much variation between individual congregations, there are two dominant ways the Bible is being read in our churches today. These two ways of looking at the Bible are mutually exclusive and there is genuine puzzlement and consternation between the two different groups of people who see such different things from the same words on the same page.

A preference for one of these two different ways of seeing the Bible is not in itself an indication of intelligence, concern for humanity or genuine faith. They are the product of church tradition, personal preference and world view. Neither way of looking at the Bible is bad or mistaken.

The problem is that this divide has created situations where there is such bad feeling that it can be impossible to sit in the same room with both views being respected. Debates have stopped being debates and have weaponised scripture, to the point that biblical verses are being used to try to win the argument, no matter what emotional and spiritual damage is caused. As Chapter 4 shows, families are being literally ripped apart. The tragedy of the current Church is that many of us exist within our own theological echo chambers and hurl insults across this theological divide to no good effect.

These two different views have created two very different reactions to the recognition of trans people within the Church. In the middle of this is a society that is losing patience with a Church that is fighting a civil war that it neither understands nor cares about, but that it increasingly feels is mean-spirited and irrelevant.

The Bible as a jigsaw puzzle

The Bible contains many stories and sayings, philosophy and rules. It is a complicated set of books that is bewildering in its complexity and its own contradictions. For example, Leviticus 11.1–31 and Deuteronomy 14.3–20 have bewildering lists of what may or may not be eaten and include many things that we would eat today. Many modern churches have added to this fragmentation by using the lectionary (a set of readings that span the Bible but do not contextualise it or produce a coherent narrative). This makes scripture for many Christians a bit like jigsaw puzzle pieces.

Consider the story of Noah and the Ark for example. Countless Sunday schools have created art, plays and songs based on an engaging story of a man who put two of all sorts of animals within a boat and saved them when God sent a big flood to wash away a sinful humanity. The end of the story is often presented as Noah building an altar and God sending a rainbow to promise never to wash away humanity again.

Most of us would struggle to tell the second half of the story. Noah plants a vineyard, makes some wine and gets very drunk and naked. Something very odd happens in his tent with his son Ham. Noah curses Ham and condemns his children to servitude in perpetuity.

Even fewer people would be able to place it within the Genesis narrative as one of the four events of the first 11 chapters of Genesis: Creation, Fall, Flood and Confusion of Tongues. Fewer still would be able to locate Noah in the lineage from Adam and Eve's third child Seth.

Yet the whole picture is important if we are going to entirely understand the story beyond a cute Sunday school story.

If we view segments of scripture as pieces of a jigsaw puzzle, scripture will give a very clear picture if all the pieces are laid down. Taking one piece of the Bible puzzle, such as the story of a man building a boat, gives us a very incomplete picture of the story of Noah.

Noah is not just a man who saves animals in a boat but also a man who will drunkenly curse his descendants to slavery for an affront to his dignity. God tries and fails to create a better humanity in Noah and his family. The richness of the story is that God continues to try to engage with all of humanity and continues to persevere.

Taking one piece of the puzzle out of the picture and insisting it is the whole picture also leaves the Bible open to being used abusively. Most people would be horrified to learn that the received wisdom during the 18th and 19th centuries was that Ham was the ancestor of all people in Africa from Egypt southwards. This was a theological justification of the slavery of African peoples. Indeed, one of the phrases used to describe enslaved Africans in the US was 'The Sons of Ham'.

We believe that this is what is happening with trans people and other sexual and gender minorities today. There is no dispute that Genesis 1, 2 and 3 deal with two differing stories of creation, and that a binary of male and female appears to be mentioned. It is also true that they are told to procreate. But these are only pieces of a much larger picture which includes the later stories of other types of people. These pieces add more to the complex narrative, all of which need to be considered.

The jigsaw approach can be a successful and rewarding way of reading the Bible. It is a method of lifelong study and constant discovery. It requires the reader to engage with every piece of the puzzle and not just to discard a piece when it doesn't seem to fit the picture. The point of any jigsaw puzzle is that you need all the pieces to make a complete picture. You cannot hold up a few pieces of the puzzle and announce you have the whole picture.

Much of the writings that have come from this approach have not been kind or helpful to trans people. They have championed some pieces of the puzzle that have included a rigid interpretation of gender and have been incurious about the rest. They have created a picture that is distorted and incomplete. But they have also robbed themselves of the richness of the greater narrative and the joy of discovery that exploration of the Bible would give them.

The mirror

The Bible can tell us much about the human condition. For example, the erotic book of poetry called Song of Solomon is an unashamed celebration of human sexuality, with phrases like *'your channel is an orchard of pomegranates with the choicest fruits'* (4.13) and *'I arose to open to my beloved and my hands dripped with myrrh, my fingers with liquid myrrh upon the handles of the bolt'* (5.5). Steamy stuff not often quoted from the pulpit.

Taking the story of Noah and using this method, we can understand that, while people can be obedient to God, no one is ever completely perfect. While we are all that virtuous builder of boats sometimes, we can also be that angry drunk who runs their mouth off thoughtlessly, sometimes with terrible consequences. This approach starts with human experience and seeks to find in the pages of the Bible a mirror to ourselves that helps us to understand ourselves and how God is present in our lives.

It also means that our understanding of scripture is heavily dependent on the society in which it is being read and the life experience of the reader. While the words may stay the same, the understandings and insights gained from scripture may be entirely different. For example, Joshua Chapter 8 details the capture of the city of Ai and the massacre of its people. For a society which is engaged in a war it may be heartening that God inspires leaders to great victories. There may be a reassurance that God will smite the enemies of good people. For those of us from more peaceful places it can be read as a series of atrocities that involve the wholesale massacre of a population and the looting and destruction of a city by invaders.

If both these responses are valid what does this do to scripture? It makes it open to many equally valid interpretations. This can be deeply troubling to people who prefer simplicity. It also raises the 'slippery slope' argument: where does this reading and interpreting stop?

The mirror method fails when we do not consider the overarching narrative of the Bible and its direction towards justice, mercy and kindness. Any action must be weighed against these biblical values.

While human sexuality in the Song of Solomon is to be celebrated, not all human sexuality is good. The abuse of God's gift of human sexuality when it is used badly and selfishly is morally objectionable. Non-consensual sex, whether it occurs within marriage or as child abuse or rape, is wrong because it does violence to another person. Coercive sex is also wrong because it uses economic, social or religious power that gives people little choice but to consent. Any time we do not treat another person as created in the image of God with equal rights we misuse God's good gift.

The disagreements about trans people are one of the many subjects that are caught up in this conflict between these two models of interpretation. The role of science, same-sex marriage and the place of women in the Church and wider society are other examples of the sharp disagreements between the jigsaw and the mirror approaches to reading the Bible.

These disagreements have led to two conversations being had in separate spaces of the Church with little genuine dialogue. Those holding the jigsaw puzzle piece view of the creation stories of Genesis are genuinely concerned that the gendered order of male headship which they read there is threatened by the idea that gender is not as it seems in their piece of puzzle. Those who use the Bible as a mirror are outraged that the human experiences of trans people, their families and the experts that work with them, are ignored and not considered in the discussions about the trans community.

The main criticism of much of the conservative (jigsaw) position is not so much that they lack empathy and compassion. The best of the writing is concerned for people and genuinely believes that trans people are hurting and seeks to provide a solution for them. The problem is that these authors are holding one or two pieces of puzzle and insisting that this is the entire picture. While they are a starting point, the two stories of creation in Genesis are not the only places that should be considered when we are seeking guidance about gender, and gender variance in the Bible, as the next section of this chapter shows.

Gender rebels in the Bible

A growing number of writers have published books that in part look for gender-variant people within the Bible. These writers include Virginia Mollenkott (2001, 2009), Vanessa Sheridan (Mollenkott and Sheridan

2003), Justin Tanis (2003), Louis Reay (2009), Victoria Kolakowski (1997a, 1997b, 2000), Linda Herzer (2016), and Deryn Guest (2006); and we did this too in our previous book *Transfaith*. All these books are listed in the References section of this book.

Rather than repeating the previous work already done, this section will attempt to summarise their writings.

Eunuchs

Many of the writers, including Mollenkott, Sheridan, Tanis, Reay, Kolakowski and Herzer, discuss eunuchs, who in both Old and New Testaments appear to be identifiably gender liminal characters. As individual characters they are often court officials. Examples include the biblical accounts of Jezebel, Esther, and the Ethiopian court official who meets Phillip on his way back from worshipping at the Jerusalem Temple and asks to be baptised in Acts 8.

Eunuchs are also mentioned in Isaiah 56 where they are promised another name and a monument better than sons and daughters if they keep God's laws. Jesus also speaks of eunuchs in Matthew 19 where he identifies three types of eunuchs; those born, those made and those who choose to be so for the glory of God. He tells people to accept this saying.

For writers who embrace the eunuch as a parallel for trans people the logic is simple: eunuchs were outside normal societal gender structures because they did not have children and were not part of the family structures that are so important throughout the biblical periods. Having renounced their allegiance, they were outside of society's traditional roles and family responsibilities.

Job

Job is a book about the nature of suffering. It is part of the Bible that we call Wisdom Literature, which is a series of books exploring philosophical questions and right ways to live. The story starts with a wager between God and Satan about a man called Job. Satan argues that Job is only pious and God-fearing because he is rich and has many children. Satan bets that Job will renounce this piety if calamity befalls him. To prove the argument, Job is afflicted with a series of misfortunes in which he loses his home, his family and his riches. He is reduced to being a beggar on a pile of ash, scraping his sores with a shard of pottery, bemoaning his fate.

Friends gather and speculate what he had done that deserved such punishment. Their speculations are based on the common assumption that such a punishment could only happen if Job had committed a great wrong. Throughout his ordeal Job insists on his innocence and refutes the increasingly nasty arguments that the group is making. He also never abandons hope in God.

At the end of the book Job is vindicated when God intervenes, showing the assumptions of his accusers are false. God also provides a glimpse of the infinite complexity of the universe, and we begin to appreciate that the simplistic ways in which humans frequently construct their arguments ignore a wider reality. Because of his faithfulness and integrity, God rewards Job with a happier life than he had had before the bet.

In *Transfaith* we noted that this narrative reflects the experience of many trans people. Their struggle with gender dysphoria, and their struggle to come out and to claim their gender, is often marked by adversity, accusation and speculation about sinfulness by other people. It is the courageous act of insisting on the truth of their own identity, and, if they retain their faith, a belief that God has not abandoned them, that transforms and frees trans people to become happy and whole people after many years of difficulty and pain.

Jacob/Israel

Herzer (2016) identifies Jacob as another gender rebel. He is the son of Isaac, and grandson of Abraham. He is the second of the twin boys born to Rebekah, clutching onto his brother's heel. As the boys grow up they couldn't be more different – Esau is the son who is big, buff and hairy, a skilful hunter and a man who lives outdoors.

Jacob is an altogether different character: a quiet man who stays close to camp doing women's work such as cooking. Indeed, his cooking skills are so accomplished that he manages to buy his brother's birth right with the bread and lentil stew he was making. We also know that he is his mother's favourite, because it is Rebekah who hatches the plot to steal her other son's blessing.

We also know that he is smooth skinned and must rely on the skin of two dead kids to give him enough masculine hairiness to deceive his father into giving him Esau's blessing. Later he has a favourite son (who is discussed below) who he dresses in ornate clothes usually reserved for virgin princesses.

While it would be unhelpful and unprovable to say that Jacob was trans, he is not exactly a stereotypical model of buff masculinity. He relies on his wits and his peculiar ability to regulate the fertility of animals to become rich and successful.

And yet he is the person who God seems to prefer. It is Jacob who encounters and wrestles with God. It is he who is renamed Israel and gives his name to a nation. It is he who is blessed twice, despite a much more traditionally masculine and forgiving brother who is the first-born son.

The key to the story of Jacob is that he refuses to let go until he is blessed. God doesn't particularly care if Jacob is smooth skinned, or he likes to hang around camp, or even that he isn't always the best brother or son. God only cares that he doesn't stop struggling with God.

And for many people this is an empowering story, that no one is beyond blessing. It is treasuring to all that God picks many different types of people to do amazing things and is open to all who are willing to hold on tight, accept unconditional love and not let go.

Joseph

Joseph is the youngest beloved son of the patriarch Jacob/Israel who is a gifted interpreter of dreams. His father favours him with an ornate robe, and between the indulgence this gift signifies, and his own arrogance towards his brothers, they hate him enough to sell him into slavery. His physical beauty lands him in trouble when he refuses to sleep with his master's wife. He is thrown in jail where he successfully interprets the dreams of two imprisoned court officials. When the reinstated official (the other is executed) needs a seer to interpret pharaoh's dreams, Joseph is sent for. He correctly interprets pharaoh's dreams and saves Egypt from famine. His starving brothers come to beg to be allowed to buy food. On their second visit Joseph reveals himself and forgives his brothers saying that God had caused his enslavement so that much good could come from it.

In *Transfaith* Joseph is identified as a gender nonconforming person. Herzer tells us that the term in Hebrew we translate as coat is *ketonet passim,* which is a term that appears only five times in the Bible.

It appears three times in the story of Joseph and the other two times it appears in 2 Samuel to describe the dress of Princess Tamar. Here is how *the ketonet passim* is described in 2 Samuel 13.18:

> Now she was wearing a long robe with sleeves for this is how the virgin daughters of the King were clothed in earlier times.

This raises many questions. Why has Jacob bought clothes that at best can be described as ambiguous in gender for Joseph? Why are the clothes suitable for a virgin princess bought and given to the youngest son? Is it the favouritism of the gift or what the gift signifies that is the real reason for the brothers' hatred of Joseph? Is this somehow related to Joseph's ability to interpret dreams? Is Joseph some kind of shaman? While no answers can be easily arrived at, they do pose fascinating questions.

Deborah and Jael

The story of Deborah and Jael appears in the times between Joshua and the establishment of the Monarchy. At that time there were a series of leaders who were called Judges.

At a time when women are considered little more than breeding property, we find the prophetess Deborah sitting in judgement and dispensing wisdom. There is no hint in this story that there is a hereditary aspect to this role; she is only described as the wife of Lappidoth.

Deborah comes up with the strategy to defeat Sisera, the leader of the Canaanite army. She is so integral to the plan that Barak the war leader refuses to go to war without her. After the defeat of his army by Deborah and Barak, Sisera flees. He meets Jael who gives him milk and curds and promises to protect him while he sleeps. In an inversion of this motherly role she hammers a tent peg through his skull, killing him.

Both women are not the standard women of the Old Testament. Herzer (2016) asks: what was it about Deborah that made her so distinct from other women that her gifts were recognised, and warriors recognised her authority? How did she see herself as she broke the boundaries imposed on her gender? Similarly, Jael takes the trappings of her only valid role in society and turns it into a deadly ruse that succeeds where the male warriors have not. Both women move out of the allowed roles for their gender with God's blessing and usher in 40 years of peace.

Lazarus (John 11)

Jesus is close to the family of Lazarus and his sisters Mary and Martha. When Jesus receives word of Lazarus' death he travels to the tomb where he is rebuked by the sisters who tell him that Lazarus would not have died if he had come earlier. Jesus raises Lazarus from the dead calling for him to emerge from the tomb. He then asks the sisters to unbind him from the strips of burial cloth that are restricting him from being able to move.

In *Transfaith* we used this story as an analogy for the trans experience. Lazarus is placed into a place of death and darkness. This mirrors the experiences of the trans people interviewed for the book prior to their coming out. They recount despair, hopelessness and very real physical danger as the statistics on self-harm and suicide show (Nodin *et al.* 2015).

Jesus calls Lazarus out of death and darkness into new life, just as many trans people feel called to live their lives in integrity and wholeness without the rejection that has blighted their lives.

It is also significant that the newly emerged Lazarus needs help to free himself from his bindings, just as the love and support of a community can help the newly emerged trans person to free themselves from the bindings of guilt, shame and secrecy that have stopped them from being able to live freely and unencumbered.

Other passages for consideration

Tamar (Genesis 38)

The story of Tamar is another part of the story of the dysfunctional family of Jacob/Israel. Tamar is wed to Er, Judah's son (and Jacob/Israel's grandson). We are told that God strikes Er dead because he is wicked. The problem for his wife Tamar is that as a widow without a son she counts for very little. Her position is made worse when Er's brother Onan refuses to do his duty to the family and have procreative sex with her so she can conceive a child who would be considered Er's son. As a strategy against conception, he ejaculates on the ground (this is often regarded as masturbation and where the prohibition against it comes from) and God strikes him dead as punishment.

Trying to save his third son from a similar fate to his brothers, Judah sends Tamar back to her family as a widow. Denied a son by Judah's family, she is of little worth. When Tamar hears Judah is travelling on a nearby road, she sees an opportunity to become pregnant. She dresses as a temple prostitute (which includes a veil to disguise her identity) and waits for Judah. She insists on easily identifiable objects (his signet ring, cord and staff) as a price for her services. Her plan is successful, and she finds she is pregnant.

When Judah hears of her pregnancy, he brings her back with the intention of burning her to death as a whore. He finds the tables have been turned when she proves by his roadside payment that he is the man who slept with her and made her pregnant. She gives birth to twin boys which means she is doubly blessed. She appears in the genealogy of Jesus in Matthew 1.

The charge of deception often raises its head in the discussion of trans people. The first UK book on trans people, by Oliver O'Donovan, makes this charge when he uses the analogy of Ananias and Saphira who defraud the growing Jerusalem church and are struck dead as a result (O'Donovan 1982).

There can be a sense of betrayal of trust for people who have known someone while they are struggling with gender dysphoria. This is particularly true when people come out as trans later in life. Often this is an intensely private struggle and the person who is undergoing it cannot name what they are feeling. Before a person comes out to those around them, there are often many small steps; first, understanding and naming what has troubled them. Next comes exploring and confirming that identity for themselves and gaining confidence to share this information. This process may last many years before someone is confident enough in themselves to share that information with everyone.

Some people can be hurt when they suddenly realise that the person who they thought they knew had hidden a large part of themselves. Yet this is not willful deception, but rather a gradual process of growing realisation and confidence. It is a strategy that allows someone to survive.

Tamar finds herself in a similar position. Unable to have a son she is just another useless widow. In her case this is made worse because she is regarded as a threat to the life of Judah's only remaining son. Her actions at the roadside are not the actions of a bad person but of a desperate woman who is trying to survive in a culture that does not value infertile widows. Her aim is to reclaim the life that had been taken away from her. Her deception is not punished as a sin like that of her husband Er and his brother Onan, or Ananias and Saphira, but rather she is doubly blessed by God with twin sons because of her actions.

The story of Tamar is one of survival, as are many of the life stories of trans people who have come out later in life. The important difference between the stories of Ananias and Saphira and Tamar is the reason for deception. One is for greed and is punished accordingly, while the other is a survival strategy which is richly rewarded by God.

Galatians 5: 16–25

Like all the letters that Paul writes to his struggling churches, Galatians starts with a problem. In this case the problem is that after he left the Galatian Church other people came to the congregation with a very different message. While Paul emphasises that there is freedom from the observances of the Jewish law and particularly circumcision, this other group of Christians comes with decidedly different ideas. The troublemakers (as Paul calls them) are insisting that Paul's message is incomplete, and that to comply with the Jerusalem Church's requirements the men needed to be circumcised.

It may have been that the troublemakers were motivated by the wish to keep the Christian message as close as possible to Judaism. Paul refers to special days, seasons and years and his frustration that they are now part of how the church organises its worship life (4.10). These are likely to have been Jewish feasts.

There is another theory that is more complex. Paul accuses the troublemakers of avoiding persecution for the cross of Christ (6.12). This is puzzling because it is a throwaway line that is not explained. Bruce (1982) outlines a fascinating theory that was first proposed by the theologian Robert Jewett.

Jewett's theory is that it was very difficult for Jews to mingle with Gentiles because there was a crackdown on it because of zealot terrorism. If everyone appeared Jewish, then it meant that the Jewish Christians would not be punished for mingling with the Gentile Christians, making it easier and safer for them.

This has direct parallels to trans people today. Several authors (Bockting, Knudson and Goldberg 2006; Bischoff et al. 2011; Chase 2011) relate how hard it is for relatives, friends and churches to deal with a loved one's transition. Other writers (Roberts 2016 and Walker 2017) have also bemoaned the difficulty in explaining the complications that trans people bring when attempting to explain gender to children. The inference these writers make is that if trans people did not live out their gender identity it would be easier for them and the other Christians whose views they champion.

Paul is clear that this seeking advantage or ease at the expense of others is moral cowardice and unfitting for a Christian. He points to his own sufferings and is clear that there is a cost to being a Christian.

Philemon

Paul writes to Philemon from prison, pleading with him to forgive his runaway slave Onesimus. In his letter Paul tells Philemon that his runaway slave has become like a son to him in his captivity. Paul insists that Onesimus is to be welcomed back and not punished in any way and that Paul will gladly pay any reparations. Paul tells Philemon it is his duty to treat Onesimus like a beloved brother because they are both one in Christ. Paul finishes the letter with a request that a room be kept ready for him – an indication that if he is freed, he will come and check that this request has been complied with. It is clearly no idle whim on Paul's part.

To understand the implications of Paul's request, we need to consider what slavery meant in the Roman Empire. Slaves were common and were essential to the fabric of society (Roth 2014). Runaways were often severely punished and sometimes killed as a deterrent to others who may have contemplated escape. Escaped slaves were considered thieves because they had stolen their mater's property – themselves.

The Roman household was headed by a paterfamilias whose word was law and who held the power of life and death over everyone under his roof. This included both biological family and slaves. Paul is asking the paterfamilias Philemon to disregard these social norms and not punish Onesimus. Even more outrageously he is asking him to treat the escaped Onesimus as an equal rather than the property without rights that he was in the eyes of the world.

In short, Paul is asking Philemon to overturn the social order because of one person. Paul is asking Philemon to do something that is unthinkable, because of love. Paul is asking Philemon to abandon his privilege and risk social disgrace because that is what Christians should do for one another.

What would that look like in our churches if we did the same? What if we took the Church's culture of deeply ingrained cisgender heteronormative male privilege and changed it out of love? What if we took the gender system that often discounts the gifts and value of women and sexual minorities and simply abandoned it because it is unloving? This is what Paul expects Philemon to do. Why should we be any different?

Using the mirror method to explore incorporating difference: The council of Jerusalem
Acts 15: 1–30

The Council of Jerusalem is one of the key moments in the new Christian movement. It was a time when two factions had two different visions for the burgeoning Jesus movement. The first was an inward-looking vision of a group of people who continued with the law as it was. This law clearly defined who was in and who was out (at least for men) because of the physical mark of circumcision. It also meant rules against eating, dressing and who you could associate with. It seems that what the Pharisees in the group wanted was for anyone who would join their movement to look like them and act like them.

This is in sharp contrast with the party of Paul and Barnabas who had been working with Gentile converts and understood that God had called these people to become part of the growing movement exactly as they were.

Like many Christians today the Party of Circumcision could go to the Scriptures and point to the requirements that God had traditionally demanded for someone to be considered a believer. They could point to the current culture of their congregations. No doubt many people liked things the way they were, and they wanted to keep them in that way.

But the party of circumcision did not win the debate. Instead, the Council decreed that the new Christians could not eat sacrificed meat from the pagan temples, strangled animals and blood. And they were to abstain from fornication. This was an enormous relaxation and revision of the laws that no doubt horrified those who kept the law in the traditional way.

Paul's Letter to the Galatians, written somewhere in the mid-first century (which may have been before the Council) speaks of the circumcision group going around and undoing what Paul had been trying to do. We know this continued afterwards as Paul's Letter to Titus, which has similar frustrations, is dated later in the 60s AD.

This argument about who is in and who is out is nothing new in the Church. Indeed, here we see that we are little different than our ancestors. They could not have seen the future, and the Jerusalem Church could not have known that much of what it held dear would soon be swept away in civil war and that they themselves would soon disappear. We cannot help but wonder whether they would have been pleased or chagrined that it was the very people they tried to exclude that carried the Church into the future.

In a similar way we cannot see the future. But we can see that parts of the Church are trying to live in a very similar way to the circumcisers by demanding assimilation of any new person and the holding of traditional ways for those who are part of their communities. We see other parts arguing like Paul and Barnabas that it is not for us to decide who God calls, but to welcome them and understand that we don't all have to be the same way.

Sometimes, like the circumcisers, we think that if we let our standards slip anything will be permissible. All groups need guidelines on how they are to live together and standards of behaviour. What we are arguing is that those guidelines and standards should not be used to exclude people from the Church any more than the Gentiles should have been excluded for not being circumcised.

It would be easy to point out that if the Council of Jerusalem had decreed the opposite way that there may not have been a Church today at all. We have the benefit of hindsight that they didn't. But if we look at the story arc of the New Testament, we see that the Good News was given to all who received it, and that it could not be contained by those who tried to use it to define who was in and who was out. This bears consideration today.

Natural Law briefly explained

Thomas Aquinas (1224–1274) believed that human beings are naturally inclined towards goodness. He thought the following five impulses were hardwired into humanity and hence were natural law:

- the need to preserve human life

- the need to reproduce
- the need to educate
- the need to live with each other
- the need to know God.

Aquinas also believed that our intentions matter; if we decide to do right, it should be because it is right and not some benefit to us. He argued that by using the God-given gift of reason, we should take these impulses and create laws and theological positions that support them. As we argue in *Transfaith,* we should always seek new information and revisit laws and theological positions to make sure that they are the best expression of protecting Natural Law.

The term Natural Law is misleading because it has the ring of the scientific about it. People assume it has a neutrality and provability. But this is not correct. It is a philosophical stance based on Aquinas's theory of what governs human behaviour and not a set of objective facts. And not all philosophers agree with the concept of Natural Law. Scottish philosopher David Hume critiqued Natural Law in his 'is/ought' fallacy. He argues that we tend to believe what is pre-existing to be natural. But this may simply not be so. Just because something currently exists does not mean that is the way it has always been intended. It simply means that this is how it is now.

Looking at the five primary precepts in relation to trans people

Natural Law has been used to object to trans people, arguing that they do not conform to Aquinas's theory. This is a particularly Roman Catholic argument (Ford 2018) based on that Church's tendency to look at history and the tradition of the magisterium, instead of biblical interpretation. This section explores the five principles in relation to trans people and seeks to counter the accusation that gender-variant people are contrary to Natural Law.

Self-preservation

As previously discussed, suicide and self-harming rates are much higher than average amongst the transgender population. Many people believe this is due to the hostile environment in which many gender-variant people live. Coming out as trans is not an act of rebellion but a desire to be able to live a life that is happy and free from trauma. Therefore, it is hard to see how trans people can be said to be in contravention of the first principle of Natural Law. It is much easier to argue that the act of coming out – and embracing the potentialities of happiness, wholeness and healing that occur when people can name who they are, and align their identity, gender expression and their bodies – is an act of self-preservation.

Reproduction

One objection to transgender people claims that they have deliberately voided the ability to procreate, but this is a misunderstanding of many trans people's lives. Some people transition well after childbearing age, others opt for non-surgical interventions. Some genderqueer people are happy to express their gender nonconformity in various ways. While it cannot be denied that some people may be unable to have children due to medical procedures used to confirm their identity, this is not universal.

In our society, some people in the Church may decide not to have children for many reasons. The Church also encourages the practice of celibacy if a person is unmarried, and some Church traditions actively encourage lifelong celibate religious vocations. It is difficult to insist that one group has a duty to procreate when this is not a universal requirement on the rest of the Church.

The education of children

Research shows that feelings of gender dysphoria manifest themselves at an early age (Conroy 2010; Dietert and Dentice 2013; Forcier and Johnson 2013; Futty 2010; Grossman and D'Augelli 2006; Kennedy and Hellen 2010). It is therefore reasonable that children are taught to name their feelings if they are gender-variant. This will help them to express themselves honestly and seek help earlier so that they can grow up with as little trauma as possible.

It is also important to educate cisgender children not to bully children who are trans. Teaching children that being transgender is wrong will do little to alleviate this situation. We need to educate children to accept themselves and be tolerant of difference. If we are taking Natural Law seriously it is hard to see how not teaching our children to name their feelings or be tolerant of others serves any greater good.

To live in society

If we believe that it is good to live in society then we must accept difference unless it is harmful. We are all different and if we are to function as a society, we need to understand that no two people are the same and that is not a bad thing. Sometimes people may say that they feel 'uncomfortable' about difference, but we may feel uncomfortable about many things without them being harmful. Being uncomfortable may even be a good thing because it helps us to learn. Being pushed to experience new things is one of the ways we grow as people.

It may be that people may feel threatened by a trans person sitting in their congregation because they have never had to think about gender before or hold a view about gender that doesn't work if they include trans people. If this is the case, we need to encourage people to own their own feelings and help them to resolve them, rather than blame someone who is merely seeking to be part of a community.

To worship God

It is highly probable that many trans people have fled the Church after hearing transphobia expressed and experiencing discrimination or abuse at the hands of the Church. It is the Church and not trans people who have violated the final precept of Natural Law by discouraging people from worshipping God. If we are to take Natural Law seriously, we should not be putting obstacles in the way of anyone who wishes to worship God.

Rules for discussing difficult topics
Matthew 15

Jesus was no stranger to religious controversy. He is frequently put on the spot by religious people for his lack of attention to the customs and rules of his society. In Matthew 15 we hear that a group of Pharisees (church leaders) and Scribes (their secretaries) come from Jerusalem with two objections. First, he is not obeying the custom of washing before eating. Second, he is taking people away from their parents, who the Law says that they must support and honour.

Jesus answers them with a quote by Isaiah which accuses them of not worshiping God, but rather human-made rules.

Then Jesus tells the gathered crowd that it isn't what goes into a mouth that defiles but what comes out of it. He points out that no matter how many purity rules are observed, all food ultimately ends up down the toilet. But he points out that words are the product of the heart. He points out that evil intentions, and by implication the words that are uttered from those evil intentions, are what defile a person.

One difficulty about the discussion that many churches have had on controversial topics is that good intentions are not always attributed to the other side of the argument.

Both sides of the argument attribute bad intentions to each other. The liberal side argues that conservative interpretations are an exercise in power, and that the motive of the institution is to simply to crush all opposition. They accuse conservatives of turning the Bible into a weapon by taking passages out of a broader context for their own ends. The conservative holds that there is a conspiracy to completely dismantle society into one big genderfluid orgy where anything goes. They also argue that the Bible is not taken seriously, if at all.

When engaging in these kinds of discussions in churches it is important to listen to why people feel the way that they do. What is it that they are concerned about? What are the assumptions? What are their fears? Are they holding a few pieces of the jigsaw puzzle and thinking it is the whole picture? Are they so concerned about justice that they feel that anything should be permissible?

It is important to get to the bottom of these questions so that we can begin to understand each other. If we do not do this, we will go away like the Scribes and the Pharisees fuming that we have been told off by each other but not really understanding the reason why we have been told off.

Listening is a difficult and naked process that asks a lot of people. It challenges us to step into a place that is uncomfortable because we are confronted with ideas we do not share and are made vulnerable by the ones we do share. It means that we must examine things that we have assumed and not examined properly and admit our own insecurities, ignorance, fear and guilt.

Much of the Church does not have this type of intimacy. Clergy fear it because it exposes them as people who often have had little time to consider how to guide their people as they labour in multiple pastorates, servicing ageing congregations, or as they try to work out new ways of attracting and retaining people in a very crowded religious market.

Congregations fear it because they are often afraid of how little they feel they know, and do not want to take the responsibility for co-creating a way forward. They feel that silent disagreement with the occasional squabble is preferable to open warfare. Denominations fear it because it may cause schism and split. It would also reduce the power of the institutional church if it were found to have been wrong all along on issues such as gender.

It is easier to agree with people who hold the same views. Change is painful and disorientating. Much of the British Church is so buffeted by societal, technological and scientific change that it feels unable to cope. As a result, much of it has retreated into proclaiming easy to understand certainty and/or tradition as a place of refuge in an uncertain world.

But we are reminded in the Letter to the Galatians that we are not here to be comfortable but to be community. That when we are sharply divided there can be no peace for anyone and bad things happen. Bad things are happening to people within the Church because we are not really talking about difficult issues such as the role of gender-variant people, but rather shouting in echo chambers and occasionally crossing swords in the media, virtual world or in print.

It's time to grow up and start listening to each other.

Chapter 3

The Culture Wars and the Christian Community

After a period where they gradually gained acceptance in most Western societies, supported by workplace protections for those who transition, and legal gender recognition in many countries, there is a growing opposition to trans people and attempts to rescind their hard-won human rights.

Becky recognised 'how much hostility there is on a daily basis' and that:

> One of the big issues is the bathroom issue in the United States and sort of demanding that people are using the loo that is the gender that they are born/assigned at birth irrespective of how well they pass or whatever changes they have made and this of course is a response of scapegoating by society and right-wing churches.

The so-called Bathroom Bills proposed in some US states, like attempts to remove trans service personnel from the US military, are examples of a backlash against trans people. Inexplicably, the former associate being gender-variant with sexual assault, and both imply that trans people represent a threat to others, with scapegoating leading directly to attempts to enact legislation against trans people. Apparently overnight (though opposition has probably always existed), trans people have become the latest targets in an ongoing culture war between progressive and conservative visions of society and the human person.

This chapter examines how these wider dynamics impact on Church life and Christian theology. The resulting tension for individuals is poignantly described by Becky:

I have really, really struggled...because I've come from such a conventional background where the rules are very clear it's been very polarised to me...there is...N's point of view where there is no such thing as transgender...you never accept it blah blah blah and she has all her literature and examples of all those people who de-transition and trans regret and all of that, so I've joined a Facebook group which is mostly American but for mothers of kids who are trans... And because I am so early in the journey here they swing massively over to the other side... It's either that you accept everything lock stock and barrel or you're some sort of evil person who is not on board with the whole thing... Really because I've been getting ever so confused about it all... And I find that all of these Facebook groups can be great, but they can become side-tracked with loads of different arguments and people can become very militant. And I'm here to say that I have a transgender child who I love and who I will support but I am not necessarily on board with everything... And that just has to be OK.

To help Becky, and anyone else who finds themselves similarly torn, the second half of the chapter considers Tina's own experiences of being drawn into these culture wars and the possibilities for an inclusive theology she discovered there. First, though, we consider the broader social context.

Women and the Church

Church congregations don't exist in a gender vacuum. As well as being set within the wider culture, churches with a nationwide reach have their own distinct denominational culture as far as gender is concerned.

Feminism, along with other social forces, has gradually improved the status of women in UK society. The extension of the franchise to women in the early 20th century was the backdrop to campaigns within British churches for the ordination of women as ministers or priests. The Methodist Church and the United Reformed Church (URC) were 'early implementers' and have included women in ordained ministry for decades. Most Congregational churches (which merged with the Presbyterian Church in England to form the URC in 1972) had been ordaining women since 1917. Methodism has a proud history of women preachers going back to John Wesley himself. The Methodist Conference in Great Britain agreed to ordain women as presbyters in 1974.

Although women's ordination was proposed in the Church of England during the early 20th century, it was 1994 before the first women were ordained as priests, and it was only in 2015 that the first women bishops were consecrated. Speaking about his positive experience as a trans person in the Methodist Church, David wondered if that was due to:

> them challenging themselves over the role of women in churches and deconstructing what womanhood is anyway and what is manhood.
> And instead of arriving at equality by keeping very defined distinct roles they have questioned what those things are anyway and that has opened them up to people who don't want to tick either of those boxes, or can't tick either of those boxes.

Anne turned this round, wondering whether:

> in some respects, having to deal with gender and sexually variant people also demands that the Church is in a good place in relation to men, women, and gender equality.

In the Church of England there are still those unable to accept women's ordination as legitimate. This is either because they believe that the Bible does not permit women in leadership (mainly held by conservative Evangelicals, for whom a literal interpretation of the Bible is determinative of doctrine), or because this is not a change that the Church of England should have made independently (mainly held by Anglo-Catholics, that is, Anglicans for whom the tradition of the Western Church, including papal teaching, is the supreme arbiter). They have been accommodated by being permitted to pass resolutions preventing women from officiating in their church or from being a member of staff. For some Anglican congregations this is such a defining issue that they also opt to come under the care of a bishop who will not ordain women. More recently still, the Church of England appointed the Bishop of Maidstone to oversee clergy and churches who adhere to the notion of male headship (see below). In the Roman Catholic and Orthodox Churches, women still cannot be priests. The institutionalising of such views by churches is making the task of equality much more difficult.

Although gender and gender reassignment are protected characteristics under the UK Equality Act 2010, faith communities have negotiated certain exemptions from its provisions, principally for employment purposes. Churches which advertise for a male priest are not breaking the law. The fact that local churches and whole denominations have obtained these exemptions means that churches do not always reflect the ethos of equality that most people have become accustomed to in their working life. This dissonance has further detached the Church from the society it claims to serve. Maria, who is Roman Catholic, commented:

> We had a bishop's letter read out the other week at a mass...asking for men to come to be deacons in the Church. Only men.
> You know it's just beyond belief...
> Unless the Church can get to the point where they are inclusive for men and women it will be a long way for trans people.

Your church and gender generally

Some of you are reading this book because you want to include transgender people in your church. If so, it's good to ask first about your congregation's attitude to gender more generally. Does your church model equality, with both women and men in leadership, or is it a congregation in which the men lead, and the women serve? Are there positive role models for both men and women? Does your church tend to segregate men and women?

Some trans people are members of churches where there are strict gender roles. Maria is active in her local Catholic church where women's roles are limited. Being transgender, as well as a woman, seems to be an added stigma. She had hoped to become a eucharistic minister – to administer communion at the Mass (women are permitted to do this) but she assumes that she is now considered ineligible because she is trans.

> We talked about it before I transitioned and then it was dropped.

Where the church segregates on the basis of gender someone's transition may or may not be perceived a problem. Some conservative Evangelical ministers have been able to accept someone who has transitioned and fits into the gender norms of the church (Marks 2009). In some of these churches transition may be assimilated into a medicalised narrative: the trans person was sick (gender dysphoric) but is now better, or a birth defect (gender dysphoria) has now been corrected. Some trans people may see their journey like that but many do not.

One the other hand, several Church of England clergy (including Tina), only transitioned as female once it had been agreed that women could be ordained to the priesthood. To have done so prior to that would probably have led to their resignation, as happened to Sally Gross[1] in the Catholic Church. Similarly, if your church's servers or choir are male-only activities, and a server or chorister begins to transition as female, their transition will be rendered problematic.

Nor should self-consciously inclusive denominations think they have nothing to learn. As David commented from his experience of the Quakers:

> some liberal churches like to think they are [welcoming to trans people] when they rarely face the situation...

Yet, it was in precisely in that kind of setting:

> that I have felt some level of exclusion so maybe it's true that the more liberal churches aren't doing as well as they think they are.

Whereas for individual congregations (here David mentioned Methodist, Anglican and non-denominational evangelical churches):

> sitting within national church bodies who are not inclusive

---

1 Sally Gross was a Catholic priest and member of the Dominican Order who had been assigned male at birth. Diagnosed as intersex when the debate about women's ordination was taking place in the Church of England, Gross was barred from priestly duties and excommunicated after deciding to live full-time as a woman (Cornwall 2010). Being *intersex* denotes a biological and chromosomal variation from the gender binary and is not the same as being transgender, which is primarily about one's sense of gender identity rather than biology (though the brain, of course, is an aspect of human biology). On investigation some trans people have been found to have an intersex condition, e.g. an extra gonad typical of the opposite sex to their assigned gender, and some intersex people transition, as Gross did.

it was important to say:

> 'We welcome you at the very least and we will campaign for our church to become better.'

We'll consider the practical aspects of including trans people in your church in Chapter 6. These examples simply illustrate the implications of variations in local understandings and national church policies concerning gender.

The Bible and the binary

In some churches a binary approach to gender (that one is born either male or female and there is no variation) is taken to an extreme. People are invited to sign up to what is claimed to be a 'biblical' understanding of manhood and womanhood that is highly prescriptive about gender roles but also surprisingly vague. The Danvers Statement on Biblical Manhood and Womanhood (published 1998) and the Nashville Statement (2017) are well-known examples.

According to the Danvers Statement, Affirmation 2: 'Distinctions between masculine and feminine roles are ordained by God as part of the created order and should find an echo in every human heart.' Affirmation 3 claims that: 'Adam's headship in marriage was established by God before the fall and was not a result of sin.'

The notion of 'male headship' is based, among other biblical texts, on a specific interpretation of St Paul's words that man is head of the woman as Christ is head of the church (1 Corinthians 11.3). In that chapter Paul appears concerned to stress the differences between men and women, in particular to regulate their behaviour on gendered lines during worship. The Corinthian congregation was a lively one in which all members expressed their spiritual gifts when they gathered in prayer. It seems that Paul felt obliged to provide these instructions to try to restrain this ecstatic community by steering it towards the gendered conventions of the day. Yet even in this chapter Paul is at pains to stress the equality of men and women (1 Corinthians 11.11–12).

A further point to note is that when Christian preachers taught mixed congregations of men and women, the women, due to lack of educational opportunities then, tended to have more questions and needed things to be explained. This interrupted the preaching. Paul's injunction (1 Corinthians 14.35) that women should ask their husbands at home ensured that the women received the education they deserved while allowing the preaching to continue uninterrupted. Women, though, were allowed to be there, which was radical by Jewish standards.

Contemporary statements on biblical manhood and womanhood treat verses that made sense in their historical context as if they were intended to apply to every subsequent era. It's true that these statements also stress the equality of men and women, with 'headship' implying a leadership responsibility within the family, workplace and church, balanced by complementary gendered roles for women. Yet beyond obvious roles as wife and mother, these gender differences are not overly defined in these statements, no doubt because modern women (accustomed to equality at work) would complain at the restrictive gender stereotyping that is implied.

Although simplistic this perspective does appear to be gaining in popularity in Christian circles, partly due to its apparently common-sense character. Unlike other societies (such as India, Pakistan or Thailand where there is a recognised 'third gender') Western society is structured on a binary model whereby you are either male or female. Yet the notion that men and women are polar opposites and complementary is a fairly modern one. It dates from the onset of industrialisation when the division between the middle-class home (female sphere) and work (male sphere) became increasingly pronounced (Shaw 2015/17).[2]

Even after two centuries of feminism, many formerly male-only professions and institutions are only now beginning to shed patriarchal attitudes and assumptions. In an era of rapid social change, clear-cut conceptions of masculinity and femininity can be attractive to some people who recall childhood or folk memories of 'the days when men were men and women were women'.

Among some Christians this binary understanding of gender has become the lens for interpreting what the Bible has to say about men and women. Genesis 1.27 is cited as a key proof text: 'So God created man in his own image, in the image of God he created him, male and female he created them.' Three points can be made in response to the idea that contemporary Western notions of the binary can be mapped on to Genesis.

---

2   The 19th-century reality was more complex, with women increasingly involved in the public sphere, as illustrated by the life and writings of Thomas Hughes, author of *Tom Brown's Schooldays* (Gill 2009).

First, while this verse acknowledges the difference between male and female, the affirmation of equality that both are created in the image of God appears far more significant theologically.

Second, as Austen Hartke (2018, p.48) has noted, Genesis says that God created 'the land and the sea' but 'there are also marshes, estuaries and coral reefs'. Far from being a list of binaries, the first chapter of Genesis offers a series of spectrums.

Third, it is extremely unlikely that ancient and modern conceptions of gender will be interchangeable. According to Fonrobert (n.d.), for example, there are at least six different words for people of indeterminate sex in ancient Jewish texts like the Mishnah and the Talmud.

Another theory, propounded by Lacquer (Thatcher 2011, pp.7–12), is that the ancient West held a 'one sex' rather than a 'two sex' understanding of the human person. Females were regarded as 'inverted' and therefore inferior versions of the male, but part of the single entity 'Man', or humanity. While this theory has not been universally accepted, it does seem to make sense of many ancient classical texts, and possibly scripture and early Christianity as well, whose focus is on the salvific nature of Jesus' humanity, not his masculinity.

Given that most people are cisgender, the gender binary works for the majority of people for much of the time. Hence the concept of two genders has rarely been questioned. It is supported by an *essentialist* understanding of gender: the presumption that only male and female exist in nature, and that each sex has inherent and distinctly different characteristics or qualities. Citing Genesis 1.27 to support this lends essentialism authority.

Some modern theologians, notably Karl Barth in the Protestant tradition, and St John Paul II, in the Catholic tradition, have interpreted the image of God in human beings in terms of a complementary understanding of man and woman. In retrospect, their ideas of complementarity appear to owe more to social conditioning than theology, but two of the 20th century's leading theologians could be referenced to support the view that men and women are equal, but essentially different.

Feminist and social theorists, notably Judith Butler (2006, first published 1990), question the essentialist view, arguing that many gendered behaviours and patterns assumed to be innate are in fact *socially constructed*. Growing awareness of gender-variant people and intersex people (assisted by the internet, which has connected hitherto marginalised groups) has made the binary idea of gender appear less tenable. While its motifs of love and relationships as explored by theologians can be aesthetically attractive, identifying the divine image with gender differences is now increasingly critiqued as a highly questionable and culturally specific move. One such critique, based on growing knowledge about intersex people, is Megan K. DeFranza's 2015 study *Sex Difference in Christian Theology: Male, Female, and Intersex in the Image of God.*

Writing nearly 30 years ago, Alistair McFadyen (1990, pp.37–38) explained:

> The image [of God] is not limited in its reference to relations between men and women... Marriage and sexual intercourse are not equivalent terms for the paradigm of 'male' and 'female'. If they were... The elderly, the impotent, the widowed, the celibate, the hermaphrodite (sic), the transsexual...would have their humanity and the humanity of their interrelationships denied them.

Although McFadyen uses terms that today, with greater knowledge and insight, have come to seem outdated or even offensive ('hermaphrodite' would be regarded as offensive by some intersex people today, as would 'transsexual' by some trans people), the important point is that he strongly affirms the image of God in both trans and intersex people. According to McFadyen, variation from the male/female binary does not prevent a person from bearing the divine image.

Contemporary statements on biblical manhood and womanhood, by contrast, are highly prescriptive about gender in their interpretation of the creation stories. According to Article 4 of the Nashville Statement, 'the divinely ordained differences between male and female' (which are not specified) 'reflect God's original creation design'. Not all Christians believe in creationism, of course, and many view trans people as examples of the normal variation apparent in nature and among human beings.

An essentialist position on gender is neatly summed up in Article 5: 'the differences between male and female reproductive systems are integral to God's design for self-conception as male or female'. In other words, one's gender must be defined by one's anatomy rather than one's sense of identity. It's an approach that works for most people but not for someone who is in any way gender-variant.

Article 6, like many conservative Evangelical statements, is fairer to intersex people[3] (though it uses a pejorative designation – not quoted here), on the ground that theirs is a physical condition, than it is to trans, gay and lesbian people, who are addressed in Article 7:

> We AFFIRM that self-conception as male or female should be defined by God's holy purposes in creation and redemption as revealed in Scripture. We DENY that adopting a homosexual or transgender self-conception is consistent with God's holy purposes in creation and redemption.

This Article assumes that trans people (and gay people) *choose* their identity – rather than receiving it as 'a given', whether by nature, or by God. Denying that trans people's experience is valid runs counter to the therapeutic consensus outlined in Chapter 1 and is considered harmful by leading specialists in the field. Although expressed as a 'firmly held religious conviction' it is not supported by current evidence about trans people's lives and contradicts best practice guidelines for their wellbeing. As 'pastoral guidance' it ignores the medical ethical principle of *nonmaleficence* or 'do no harm'.

Gender ideology

Catholic[4] statements about the family and marriage often lament *a gender ideology* at work in society that is said to undermine both. The expression 'gender ideology' is a stigmatising term applied to people whose households are not heteronormative and is a classic example of the confusion of gender identity with sexual orientation. *Heteronormativity* includes the belief we have just been critiquing: that there are only two genders – male and female – each of which has complementary roles, assigned by nature (or God). It also regards heterosexuality as the norm for everyone, and sex and marriage as the exclusive preserve of two people of the opposite sex.

---

3   George noted 'the paradox…that in the Greek Orthodox Church there is an affirmation ceremony for people who are intersex, and they have been identified as more than one gender' but nothing equivalent for trans people.

4   Camosy (2018) reports that Catholic ethicist Professor David Jones is developing theological and pastoral resources that involve dialogue with clinicians and transgender people, an approach we advocate.

Trans people often assume that the phrase 'gender ideology' refers to them. The real target (though it can be opaque in Vatican and Bishops' Conferences' statements) is likely to be married gay and lesbian people whose relationships are presumed to detract from heterosexual marriage. If they have children, their family life is reckoned to be deficient because child-rearing is said to require both a father and a mother, even though the evidence contradicts this claim.

Inadvertently trans people are being drawn into a culture war around same-sex marriage as objections shift from sexual orientation to the construction of gender in lesbian and gay relationships and families.[5] Austen Hartke (2018, pp.13–15) reports the role of 'three powerhouses of conservative Christian social action' in the US who have 'been instrumental in influencing legislative efforts against transgender Americans'.

Anne noted that sexuality and gender identity have become increasingly confused in the current culture wars:

Traditionally the Catholic Church has always assumed that gender identity must conform to sex and that appears throughout the doctrine even with Pope Francis...there is a very anti separation element and you're seeing this to extremes in the States and places like that and culturally in a way with people in society.

It's generally assumed that gender and sex go together it seems obvious... When in fact people haven't met transgender people or LGBT people...the presumption is... These issues are in the pursuit of desire and the reward of inappropriate sex.

Ed recalled the Church's role in reinforcing heteronormativity:

The thing I found difficult about the Church growing up was it was very much this trajectory set for you 'that this is your gender and therefore this is the sexuality that you will have and...this is God's purpose for your life for you to marry and blah blah blah.'

---

5   A high-profile US example is Ryan Anderson, the author of several books opposing equal marriage, and more recently *When Harry Became Sally: Responding to the Transgender Movement* (2018). Like Paul McHugh (see Chapter 1 above), whom he quotes extensively, Anderson is a Catholic.

For him, Christian heteronormativity appeared totalising and verged on idolatry:

> And I think it is so deeply worshipped by places in the Church that it can be quite difficult... There is no alternative to that that is even explored so for me in my head it was what I had to do and there was no other choice around that yeah...
> No alternative so I feel that was kind of quite drummed in.

In the firing line

While opposition to same-gender marriage is the official position of many Christian denominations (though not Baptists, Quakers, the United Reformed Church and others in the UK) the churches have effectively lost the argument as the UK now practises equal marriage. As a consequence, religious opposition has become more concentrated, and vocal. There has also been an increasing pushback against the basic human rights of trans people and other minorities. Some of this hostility has come from what, to many, seems a somewhat surprising direction: radical, lesbian feminists. To elucidate, we'd like to tell a true story that involved Tina.

> In the summer of 2018, a row erupted about the women's only pond at Hampstead Heath in London. A spokesperson for the Lesbian Rights Group objected to trans women swimming in the pond, but she didn't use the term 'trans women'. She spoke instead about 'men who identify as women' which implies, as intended, that trans women are men pretending to be women. I (Tina), when interviewed about this on the BBC London news, pointed out that the objector appeared not to understand trans people's experience. A spokesman for the City of London Corporation (who manage the pond), quoted what had been said robustly by the Women and Equalities minister, Penny Mordant, when launching the 2018 consultation on the proposed revision of the Gender Recognition Act 2004: 'Trans women are women, and trans men are men.'

The notion that the trans people might not be, or are not, who they say they are, stems partly from a (sometimes deliberate) misunderstanding of the concept of self-declaring one's gender identity that was at the core of the 2018 consultation. What was proposed was a gender recognition pathway that is less dependent on doctors and medical documentation, in line with the de-pathologising of gender variance noted in Chapter 1. What self-declaration emphatically does *not* mean is that a male bodied person can announce and gain legal recognition that they are a female yet continue to live as a male. The proposals still envisaged the requirement (also in the 2004 Act) that applicants would swear a legally binding oath to live out their days in the gender to which they had transitioned.

That a few second wave radical feminists[6] are increasingly vocal in denying trans women's reality, and access to women-only spaces, has come as a shock, but the attitude is not new. The perception that trans women are really men who colonise women's spaces was one thesis of US author Janice Raymond's 1979 book, *The Transsexual Empire*. She argues that those who were socialised as males have enjoyed male privilege and can never understand what it is to be a woman. This ignores the fact that trans women experience their childhood or adolescence differently to cisgender male bodied people. (It's a common misconception that trans people know what it's like to live as (cis) male or (cis) female, and many don't know what it's like to live as either gender.)

Other radical feminists, like Andrea Dworkin and Catherine MacKinnon, argue that transition helps to reinforce both gender stereotypes and patriarchy, although they have welcomed the anti-patriarchal potential of severing the link between biology and destiny that trans people's experience represents. For some trans people, of course, transition can entail the acquisition of hyper-feminine or hyper-masculine gender presentation, whether from personal choice, social or clinicians' expectations, or a desire to pass unobtrusively and safely.

Like her successors today, Raymond says little about trans men, beyond that they are traitors to the cause of women's equality. Her arguments do not stand up well against the vastly improved knowledge about trans people's reality since she wrote. Others, like Germaine Greer, still hold an essentialist understanding of gender, and their

---

6   First wave feminism describes women's struggle for equality, especially for the right to vote during the 19th and early 20th century. Second wave feminism began in the 1960s and aimed to liberate women by a radical critique of sexist assumptions that inhibit women's equality in the workplace and education. It was assisted by the development of the contraceptive pill.

views of trans women remain unchanged. Writers Julie Bindel and Julie Burchill use forceful, inflammatory language to express their position, and their opponents have coined the term TERF – trans exclusionary radical feminist – to describe it.

These antagonistic attitudes have aroused equally impassioned and verbally violent responses from trans people, and unedifying Twitter wars that have done neither group any favours. The exclusionary narrative is almost always about trans women rather than trans men, though the latter are indirectly affected by it. This may be related to some trans women's higher visibility due to lasting, or not easily altered, effects of a male puberty. If so, it looks like a form of bullying. There is also evidence (Morrison 2010) to show that trans people can be embattled on two fronts at the same time, with radical feminist criticism on the one side, and poor attitudes from some members of the lesbian, gay and bisexual community on the other.

Another anti-trans narrative targets trans children and adolescents, claiming that they are being fast-tracked into altering their bodies when, in fact, their care is conservatively and carefully managed by professionals. Often the parents are blamed, adding further stress to families already coping with the complication of caring for a transgender child.

For over three decades between 1970 and 2004, UK trans people lived in a legally anomalous position, unable to have their birth certificates amended to reflect their transition. This era started with the 1970 *Corbett v Corbett* ruling that trans woman and model April Ashley was not a woman for the purposes of marriage. This legal anomaly ended with the passing of the Gender Recognition Act in 2004. During that period there was the occasional questioning of trans people's status, like Germaine Greer's unsuccessful opposition to trans woman Dr Rachel Padman being admitted as a Fellow of Newnham College, Cambridge in 1996. Trans man Mark Rees (2009, first published 1996, pp.154f), however, was unable to enter the discernment process for ordination in the Church of England in the era before women could ordained as priests, as according to his birth certificate he was legally still a woman.

As far as we're aware, there were no major UK attempts to exclude trans women from women-only events, like that in the early 1990s at the Michigan Womyn's Music Festival in the US – which subsequent organisers of the event have apologised for. More recently, trans people's right to access (with limited exceptions) single-gender facilities has been protected by UK equality legislation. Tensions may arise though, and even Christian feminists can find themselves conflicted, as in this next story, where the tensions are overcome by a Christ-like action. This narrative inspires the trans inclusive theology that follows.

Crossing the barriers of hostility

In 2008, I (Tina) attended a women-only Christian retreat drawn by its subject matter, the link between dance, movement and spirituality. On the first morning some of the women expressed anxiety that the group's female space was being threatened by another resident in the retreat house. (It later transpired that this was a trans woman at the very beginning of her transition.) Although I myself had transitioned some years earlier, this response made me nervous and I spoke to Anita [not her real name], one of the older women in the group, about my own journey. Later that day Anita told me that she had invited the other trans woman to dine with her that night and that they would be seated at a separate table from me and the other retreatants. She also explained that this person was at the start of her transition and that it was important for me to meet with her during the weekend, which I did.

Anita was hugely assured in responding to and resolving what had been, until that point, a troubled scenario. This was partly due to her seniority and also, presumably, her sense that to eat with the trans woman was the Christ-like thing to do. Sharing a table together that evening demonstrated to the other women that they had nothing to fear from this person who was, in fact, at the very least a friend, and possibly their sister.

Without knowing the person, or their circumstances, the group had rendered them a dangerous 'other' and objectified them as an 'alien' to be denied welcome or hospitality in their circle. Reactions like this arise spontaneously, but if not reflected upon, easily consolidate, particularly when they awaken hidden fears and anxieties. To have confronted these negative feelings directly would have been painful for a Christian group, for whom hospitality towards the stranger is a virtue.

By dining with the ostracised person, Anita offered them love and hospitality. She demonstrated to the whole group that this is how Christians should behave, not just to one another, but to those who are inhabiting a community's margins.

Care of the alien and stranger, strongly emphasised in Old Testament texts (Exodus 22.21; Deuteronomy 10.19), 'because you too were strangers in the land of Egypt', is enacted by Jesus in his ministry at the margins: healing the mentally ill and lepers; dining with tax collectors and sinners. It is a ministry that invites derision: Jesus is dismissed as a law breaker, a wino and a glutton. It also invites awe that someone would risk both religious disapproval and the stigma associated with the marginalised, by coming close to them. Yet the gospels tell us that this is what Jesus did, and his stigmata are only complete when he endures crucifixion, the common punishment of the common criminal in his day.

The parable of the Good Samaritan recorded by St Luke (10.30–37), ostensibly about acting as a neighbour across ethnic and religious borders, has traditionally been read as a vignette of Jesus' own ministry. Rabbi or teacher to his disciples, Jesus is not a religious official like the Levite or priest, but more of an outsider, like the Samaritan, who was ethnically and religiously 'other' according to his Jewish hearers' preconceptions. Yet priest and Levite keep their distance from the body at the roadside, for good religious reasons. It is the Samaritan who crosses over, risking danger, contagion and ritual impurity. It is he who tends the traveller's wounds, pouring in oil and wine. Jesus too broke down the barriers between the pure and the impure, the inner circle and those at the periphery. The Samaritan generously supports the man's continuing recovery and Jesus' ministry too will be costly – for him.

On this interpretation of Jesus' parable, the Samaritan can represent pastoral care by the trans ally. Not all, but some, trans people may be deeply wounded by their journey, especially when rejected by family, friends and colleagues. Other trans people will have experienced physical attack as well, like the man mugged on the road from Jerusalem to Jericho. Ministry in these circumstances may make demands on minister and community, and require gentleness, compassion and time before wounds begin to heal. When this happens, you will need to find the courage to be a true ally to the trans person concerned.

Ministry, though, is never simply one way, and the 'wounded' can themselves bring healing to others. Indeed, an alternative interpretation of the parable would be to see the trans person, not as 'the victim' on the road, but as the Samaritan: apparently 'other' simply because of their gender identity, but someone in whom the grace and love of God are abundantly at work. Jesus' parable seems to have been designed to overcome his hearers' prejudices and convey how much we have to learn about ourselves by engaging with those who seem to differ from us.

Three other Lucan parables (15.3–32), the lost coin, the lost sheep and the prodigal son, also convey Jesus reaching out to those who were (literally in the case of the younger son) missing from the table. Both in his parables, and in what the gospels tell us about what Jesus taught and did, his was a mission to seek and save those currently excluded from community, helping them to know that God's kingdom was among them too.

In the parable of the prodigal son, the father is not simply pleased to see him, but celebrates his return by treating him almost as if he were his sole heir. Since the youngster has already squandered his own share of the inheritance, this annoys the one whose due it is, his stay-at-home elder brother. In vain the father pleads with the older son to share his happiness at his younger brother's return. Within the context of the early Church, these details are assumed to depict the tensions between orthodox pharisaical Judaism (the elder brother) and 'the unrespectable kind of Jew who became a Christian' (the younger brother) (Drury 1973, p.156).

Taking Jesus' ministry as the paradigm for our own suggests that ministers and churches should be proactive in working out their theology, and the practice that follows from it, rather than waiting for trans people to turn up and then trying to see how they might fit in with an existing ethos.

If your theology leads you to celebrate trans people's lives, rather than merely tolerating them (and the ministry of Jesus does appear to point in that direction) then some people, like the elder brother in the parable, may well moan and grumble that 'it's not fair' or 'it's not right'. Theology and practice that reflect the nature of God as we see it in Jesus will disturb and unsettle as it breaks down barriers of suspicion and inequality. Inclusive theology is costly rather than cosy! Now though we'd like to tell another story.

'Fancy a swim?' The Baptismal
basis of inclusive theology

The night that I (Tina) appeared on the local television news item about trans women and the women-only pool, an email dropped into my inbox with the subject 'Fancy a swim?' The sender, a woman who had swum in the women-only pool for several years, invited me to join her 'not as a protest or demonstration, but so that you can come and enjoy the water.' I was very touched by this and met the sender for coffee (rather than a swim!). The woman did not have a religious faith. Her motivation for writing was that she objected strongly to the notion that one group of people claimed ownership of the pool. She had witnessed another woman in the pool telling a trans woman 'you shouldn't be here' and challenged her behaviour. Hence, she reached out with an invitation during the latest row. This episode reminded me of a women-only event in January 2012, organised by the Cutting Edge Consortium, a network of faith and belief (non-religious) groups opposed to homophobia and transphobia. Shocked to discover that trans women were being excluded from women-only events, the organisers invited me to be on the panel and the publicity emphasised that this event was for 'everyone who identifies as a woman'.

In fact, I was reluctant to take up the invitation to go for swim, even though the policy stated that I could, and my new friend would be beside me. By promoting fear, the exclusivist position, although mistaken and harmful, is often successful and many trans people are reluctant to enter our churches for this reason. No one wants to be rejected, especially if it has happened before, so some trans people may need a great deal of coaxing before they can even begin to try church again.

'Fancy a swim?' The invitation evokes the water of the pool or pond – its depth and refreshment – companionship, and theologically, the sacrament of baptism. In churches where the baptism of children is the norm, one can easily overlook the important role of sponsors for adult candidates, and of the catechetical journey, in which someone more experienced in the Faith nurtures the candidate, leads them to the baptismal waters, and continues to support them on the other side of the font.

A trans inclusive theology needs to find embodiment in guardians of the openness of sacred space, who are unafraid to challenge those who impose false limits; people with an inviting manner, ready to accompany the trans person, whether baptised or unbaptised, as they splash in the shallow end of their new community.

A Taizé icon of the Baptism of Christ (which is behind my (Tina's) desk as I write) depicts the Spirit descending as a dove – a reminder of the gift of the Holy Spirit in baptism – and below the figure of Christ, Adam and Eve swim among the fishes in the River Jordan! Their primordial freedom, once so tragically lost, seems restored at last, along with the divine image, as Christ is proclaimed, 'Beloved Son'.

All human beings need to love and to be loved, and sin is mostly the failure to love. Baptism is the sign that we are, to use the King James translation, 'accepted in the Beloved' (Ephesians 1.6). Baptism is also the basis of the Church's life and ministry. It was by paying close attention to the theological and ecclesiological implications of the baptismal covenant, that the Episcopal Church in the United States made such huge strides with the inclusion, first of women in the Church's life and ministry, and latterly lesbian, gay, bisexual and trans people.

Inclusion in the Church for one group of people means inclusion for everyone, not simply on the rational, secular ethical principle of equality, but because of what it means to be a full member of the Church through baptism.

Steve describes the baptismal formula Galatians 3.27–28 as 'the classic verse' and 'helpful':

> For as many of you as were baptised into Christ have put on Christ. There is neither Jew nor Greek, there is neither slave nor free, there is neither male nor female; for you are all one in Christ Jesus.

A biblical passage with huge meaning and relevance to the struggle for the full inclusion of women in ordained ministry (see Schüssler Fiorenza1994, first published 1983), it is also loved by and significant for trans (and also intersex) Christians as a theological foundation for their affirmation within the Body of Christ.

Schüssler Fiorenza's (1994, first published 1983, p.218) feminist reading of this verse is that early Christianity had an egalitarian self-understanding of 'the oneness of the body of Christ, the church, where all social, cultural, religious, national and biological gender divisions and differences are overcome and all structures of domination are rejected'. Yet it appears to have been quickly modified by the idea that a women's gender is erased by her baptism, her union with Christ, and her participation in his body, the Church.

The notion that baptismal identity in Christ erases one's gender identity often arises in Church discussions about rites for trans people. It can be a way of dismissing trans people's experience by implying that their gender identity has been erased by their baptism. Aspects of our identities that keep us in bondage, such as racism or sexism, are broken by our baptism into Christ, but the effect is to enhance who we are, rather than to belittle, or render someone invisible.

Liturgies co-created by trans people and their clergy often include the renewal of baptismal vows, thereby linking the trans person's unique journey with their pledge to follow Christ. Trans people who were baptised as children may wish to renew their baptismal vows, and to receive a certificate in their current name, which reflects their gender identity. In very conservative churches even this can be problematic, as George explains:

> These are things of great importance... I have tried to find someone to help me through the official routes... I can't find anyone and if supposedly there is such a person they will never get OK from the bishop, the archbishop, whatever.

It would be simply 'out of the question', despite emphasising the continuity of the person's Christian identity.

Not all rites co-created by clergy and trans people include the renewal of baptismal vows. Some focus on a name change, or the celebration of a gender identity, previously hidden but now being claimed. When Church governing bodies discuss liturgical provision for trans people, they tend to focus on their Christian identity and renewal of their baptismal faith. The sacrament of Christian equality, baptism neither precludes, nor erases, particular identities or specific needs within the Body of Christ. What these needs might be for trans people's loved ones and for trans people themselves is the subject of the following chapters.

Chapter 4

Loving Someone Trans

Introduction

This chapter reports the findings of two group interviews that were designed to give a snapshot of the cares and concerns of those who are directly and intimately affected by the gender journey of a loved one. This chapter has several parts:

- two points related to our methodology (which is described more fully in the Introduction)

- a summary of the findings of the interviews

- a reflection of what these findings tell us about the pastoral and spiritual needs of those who journey with loved ones as they transition and live beyond the end of their transition.

A critical observation to bear in mind when reading this chapter is that we firmly believe that gender variance is simply part of the wonderful diversity of God's creation. But we also believe this diversity has not been addressed with sufficient justice, empathy and kindness. The difficulties experienced by the families in this chapter were not inherent in the fact their loved one is trans. Society, and particularly the Church, are often difficult and hostile places for trans people to come out in. This difficulty and hostility creates situations of distress for families as they come to terms with a loved one coming out as trans.

This is borne out particularly with the two partner interviews, where both are in supportive spiritual and social spaces. In both interviews the young partners often seemed puzzled by the stories of distress and pain the parents related. These partners spoke of adjustments to their relationships as their partner transitions, rather than problems.

We believe that this is the future. As society and the Church become more trans-friendly much of the pain and anguish caused by the gender journey will simply disappear. Healing does not need to happen if no wounds have been inflicted. If young trans people are supported, nurtured and loved, to the point where transition is seen as simply part of a personal journey of discovery, it may be that in the future very little particular pastoral care is needed.

More about method
Conversation style and transcription

The conversations occurred between parents and partners and they were able to talk freely about their own stories with very little direction from us beyond a general prompt to:

- tell their stories

- tell what helpful or unhelpful behaviour they had experienced from their faith communities

- tell what they would value from ministers or pastoral carers as people who love someone who is gender-variant.

Limitations

This was a small sample of people who have been recruited from places where trans people are loved, welcomed and affirmed. This chapter does not purport to be exhaustive in its insights and findings, but is designed to help those seeking to offer pastoral care to those affected by the gender journey of loved ones by offering some insights that they might find helpful.

It is not an exhaustive study, which is beyond the scope of this book, and we recommend that a much larger research project exploring these relationships would be incredibly useful and important.

What the parents said in their focus group
Initial reaction and support received by parents

The background of the parents made an impact on how they received the news of transition. Becky was from a more conservative background and openly struggled to reconcile what she had been told by her church about trans people with the love of her child. As she puts it:

> So my son came out as being gay when he was 16...but when he was 17 he came out as transgender and wanted to transition. ...She is now 20 and she has transitioned. ...It has been a minefield for me... absolutely... I was horrified if I am honest... This doesn't feel very politically correct to say...it was dreadful. It was hard enough [him] being gay because I come from a strict Baptist background...my father has died now but he was a pastor.

Nothing had remotely prepared her for the situation in which she found herself. Coming from a conservative background there had been little or no theological understanding besides the idea that being trans was sinful, aberrant behaviour that could be cured through prayer, and a refusal to accept the situation under any circumstances. Similarly, theology was presented as a series of propositions to believe rather than a set of ideas to be explored and critiqued. As such she was theologically and psychologically unprepared to support herself or her child.

What compounded this difficult situation was that her primary support networks were socially conservative Christians and they were unable to help her deal with the situation she found herself in.

> And it was never spoken but the shockwaves I felt to be...Becky's grandchild is transgender. ...You know it was such, such a massive thing... No one had ever come across it before...nobody had... And I just felt like my child was a just this pariah... This leper.

Her church struggled to come to terms with the situation and avoided the issue wherever possible. While outright condemnation would have been worse, it was extremely unhelpful that the minister charged with pastoral support also completely withdrew his presence.

> It felt like it was the worst thing that had happened to anybody, it was the worst...it was unmentionable.
>
> I can count the conversations I had on one hand with various people. ...So I contacted the pastor of the church and he was like so shocked. He was like 'Oh I'll get back to you I don't know much about this.' And after that he would pretty much run away from me... If I saw him at church, he would just totally ignore me. ...And some people would say my child will be very welcome in church...and I thought like yeah...

At the very time that she and her child needed the support from her church and minister there was complete failure to care or to provide support. Indeed, she only found alienation and condemnation:

> As far as they are concerned there is only positive outcome – for my child to de-transition – and unless that happens there is no good that can come of that life at all. And that hurts, that really hurts...

After receiving little support from the church, Becky felt invalidated herself so she left. There was no follow up:

> I'd been there for years... They'd seen the kids grow up and then they... We walked out of there and not one person phoned me... You know it was like we'd completely ceased to exist...and we've been in what is their [church] family.

This contrasts sharply with Sophie's experience:

> For me this was also difficult...new territory...unknown situation...
> I was incredibly supported by my family and by my congregation. I'm a Quaker and Friends are very, very, receptive and open in this situation and they helped us immensely... They realised straightaway I needed help...

The faith community helped by creating a safe space where Sophie could work out and come to terms with her child coming out:

> First of all, what helped me was that this was a place where I could bring the whole story... I didn't have to hide and there was some room... at a national level I had come across some prominent people who were within the church – we call them Meetings – who were trans openly so as a well-known fact. That first of all they said that this was an OK thing to be happening...and that was comforting... That was a safe place to be.

This help came in many ways including the ability to create a safe place for the family when they needed time to absorb the information, a place to explore and discuss, a place to be reassured and a place where there were role models that pointed to a positive and possible future.

The faith community also provided practical help such as providing a safe place for respite:

> He decided to go to live...we didn't know how long for, but it turned out to be six months from the age of 16-and-a-half to 17 with this elder and her husband who were absolutely marvellous... They never made any judgements, asked no questions, they just opened their home and made a safe place for our son to be and we could go and be with him as much as we wanted to...
>
> So it created some space so... It gave him a place where he was safe and eventually when he felt ready he would come back home...
>
> And our journey continued, and the Meeting has been there all the way through...

Coming from a tradition that has been at the forefront on issues of faith and diversity, it was easier for Sophie's faith community to be a supportive space for the family as they began the gender journey together. As she relates:

> There is an African saying that it takes a village to bring up a child. And I feel it took the whole Meeting to bring up mine. He was as much their achievement as mine. As a family they have got him there and I am so grateful to them yeah... The depth of happiness and connection with him...you know the whole community...they came from that acceptance and support.

The contrast between the two experiences could not have been more extreme. It is likely that one of the factors that created these contrasting experiences is the way that theology is done within the two different faith communities. In Becky's case there was a strict theological setting with little room for doubt or open discussion, and the only response, short of outright condemnation, was silence. This contrasts sharply with the Quaker way of doing theology as Sophie recounts referencing the conversations that took place around same-sex marriage.

> When we were at the annual yearly gathering of Quakers in Britain that affirmed same-sex marriage on an equal terms as heterosexual marriage...before the law changed so that [we were] then advocating

and campaigning for that change... There was a lot of people who came in thinking we can recognise committed partnerships, but you know marriage is a word too far...by and by the end of the week by listening to people's experiences we recognised that marriage is the Lord's business and we are nothing but witnesses meaning that we only can recognise God's work in someone else's life, it's not our doing... We don't bestow that... What we are doing is to recognise when we see marriage it is marriage.

What is striking about these stories is that both parents started in a place of confusion when their child came out as trans. What makes the difference in the unfolding stories is how the faith communities reacted; the first exacerbated the trauma of the situation by withdrawing critical support at the time it was needed, which also meant that the parent was left alone and unsupported. While it is not possible to prove, the reaction of the church can be interpreted that they hoped if they ignored the problem it would go away, which it did.

The second faith community acted as a support network and turned the situation into an opportunity to show support and uncritical love. The effect was that the family was even more connected to its faith community with deeper bonds created through a shared journey of discovery and learning.

In the interview the impact of what had happened was most noticeable in the way these stories were told. Becky spoke in tones of anguish about the pain and trauma of her situation which bought the entire group to tears. Sophie told her story calmly, often with a smile, as she recalled a difficult but rich time where she and her family were held, supported and nurtured by their faith community.

Impact on family relationships

Both parents related that there had been strain in their marriages as they struggled to support their child. Becky found that her marriage broke down completely:

I was in my second marriage... And the little church I went to... And my sister gave me and my husband the advice that we must never ever accept or affirm this transition. ... And basically, my husband kicked my child out. Then my children, both of them in solidarity, went to live with their dad... So I lost my kids back in 2015...

My marriage didn't last after that obviously.

Sophie related how the respite provided by the Quaker meeting provided the space needed to both come to terms with the situation and also the strains that it created in the marriage:

So, it created some space... And so my husband and I could work on our marriage, which was perilously [laughs] close to the rocks because we were so emotionally exhausted, and we couldn't support each other in all this...

So we were going through a difficult time... And it helped...it made space...

It is not possible from the interviews to guess the solidity of the interviewees' marriages prior to the child coming out as trans. But what is evident from the two different accounts is that where there was a supportive environment that allowed the parents space and time to absorb the reality of the situation; where they were allowed space to support each other, communicate and heal, the marriage survived. Where this did not happen, the marriage failed.

It should also be noted that it was the rejection of Angela (Becky's daughter) that led to the disintegration of the entire family. In the act of expelling the trans child from the home, Becky's husband created a situation where the rest of the family had to choose sides. In this case all the immediate family members chose to support their child or sibling. This meant the family unit was unable to survive the coming out of the young trans person. While the coming out was a catalyst, it was the banishment of the child that was the trigger for the family breakup.

These interviews also indicate the impact on the other children in the family. Sophie related that while the whole family were engaged in the support of their trans son, the other son suffered. This was because their preoccupation with their trans son meant that they were unable to focus on the very real needs of their other son who found the situation very difficult. Sophie recognises that they did not give him the support he needed, particularly after the incident where he was the person who discovered David had made a suicide attempt:

My other son's story...

And you know he is a 32-year-old man now who was a few weeks ago was weeping uncontrollably because he has not processed the trauma of being the first one [to find his brother after he made a suicide attempt]...

When he [David] took the overdose and he had to wait for me to arrive thinking that his brother, sister then, was going to die so... He has the trauma that is now coming out in depression and anxiety and other things and he needs support.

I realise when we were struggling to support our trans son we neglected to support him so...10 years on, and even with all the good things and blessings, there is still work to be done...

So everyone is involved when these things happen, not just the person... It is...there is a lot of collateral damage.

These actions cannot help but bring trauma to a family that is already dealing with the coming out of their family member. David's brother was the first person to discover a suicide attempt and this has scarred him deeply. In such difficult situations the distress caused by the actions of their trans siblings, and the lack of capacity to focus on their own needs, are likely to have a negative impact on those children's own wellbeing.

Becky relates the ongoing difficulties for one of her daughters when she is in public with her transgender sister, Angela:

And I have been able to talk with my other daughter. I have a 17-year-old daughter. We struggle, and it was interesting to hear about... She needs support because it has been really hard for her socially when we go out with Angela. Angela's become quite flamboyant and sort of... There's been quite a lot of changes and it's been a coping strategy... strategy to cope with stuff and...

Poor lass she is the most socially conservative kid... You know she has to be the same as everyone else and she isn't able to be embarrassed... She's only 17 and she finds it excruciating sometimes going out with her big sister no matter how much she loves her...

These quotes bring up several important points about the impact on siblings when a child in the family transitions. First, much of the focus of the parent's energy is on helping their trans sibling through the initial difficulties of transitioning. Sophie acknowledges that while they tried their best, the gender journey of one son was a cause for trauma for the other. It is only with hindsight that she realises the support and help that the cisgender son needed to help him understand and accept the situation was not there when it was needed. This has had a negative impact on his life in the form of depression and anxiety.

For Becky, the coming out of her daughter as trans led to the disintegration of the family unit itself. The children not only had to make sense of the marital breakdown, but also had to make sense of the gender journey of their sibling. Becky's quote about her other daughter's reaction to being seen publicly with her sister echoes this sense of unease. As a teenager wishing to fit into her conservative peers' social network she is placed in a difficult situation as she walks a difficult path of trying to fit in and support her sister simultaneously.

This section acknowledges the uncomfortable fact that when a child comes out as trans, the whole family is affected. Pastoral care cannot simply focus on the person coming out – the faith community needs to support the entire family as they begin to participate in the gender journey of their loved one.

For all those affected by a loved one's gender journey it is likely to be the first time they have encountered a world hostile to gender-variant people. For the first time they see the effects of this hostility and how it begins to play out in the lives of their family. They need help and a safe place to come to terms with this as much as with the fact they have a family member who is trans.

Grief

It is impossible to leave this discussion without considering grief. Literature on the topic includes Norwood (2012) who finds that the reaction of family members to someone coming out as trans is a complex process involving grief for something that is akin to death.

This sense of grief was echoed in both the interviews. Becky stated in the interview:

> So that doesn't help me with grieving...because I'm perpetuating that myself you know... Oh, I miss my little boy... And I do miss my little boy and that's just it.

and:

> Me and her...are going through this grieving process... Honestly it
> would be easier if my child had died... So that's that.

And Sophie adds:

> Yes, my child had died...the child I thought I had and now he was alive
> again in a different way, just like on the road of Emmaus... You may not
> recognise him at first but then something reveals that this is the same
> person. ...It is not a new person it is the same person but he has kind
> of a different more precious life coming through him...

Both the literature on the subject and the voices of the parents agree
that a child coming out as trans creates a feeling of loss. While it could
be argued that all children rarely live up to the expectations and dreams
of parents, this is particularly true of people who transition across
the gender binary. The name given by parents and all the gendered
expectations of the future are discarded in the reality of the revealed
gender identity of their child.

This loss is exacerbated as the trans person begins to confirm their
gender identity and their physical appearance begins to change. In this
sense the Emmaus quote from Sophie is particularly helpful: while the
parent may not automatically recognise their child as they transition,
through interacting and journeying with them they begin to recognise
the person that they have always loved.

It is also important to see that this grief can have a resolution.
Angela's gender journey began less than three years ago and is still
ongoing. Becky is still adjusting to this as she tries to reorient her life
in a new church and as a single woman. For Sophie the events that she
described happened over a decade ago and during this time healing and
reflection have replaced grief with a sense of wonder:

> What our friend here said about there being no male or female in Christ
> or God is very important to me and that was one of the first glimpse
> of what I would call seeing God's glory in that...in the shape of my son
> and his story...understanding that God makes no mistakes and the fact
> that there are people who have intersex conditions and have different
> expressions of gender and sexuality is all part and parcel of this big

mystery which we call God, Life with a capital L – substitute whatever works for you...

So for me that's part of revelation it's not just what's happened... if somehow, it's just about this terrible thing that happened... It is the cracking open of the shell which makes it possible for me to glimpse beyond what was already known so it is part of my spiritual growth... deepening...flowering...call it what you like this experience.

So it's not sort of happenstance that I just have to put up with or tolerate it is what makes me who I am... In the same way giving birth made me a mother, giving birth to my trans son has taken that motherhood to a different level and a different place that is entirely spiritual...

So that there are things of the flesh and things of the spirit and that the experience for me has been the...you know...taking me out of my comfort zone and flinging me into a place where I can see a God that I couldn't have seen without this.

Concluding comments

What is striking about these two accounts is that the outcomes they describe are completely opposite. For Becky, the coming out of their child created a disruption that destroyed a family unit and alienated her from her faith community. In the story of Sophie, we find the opposite: a family, although disrupted, was able to come to terms with what had happened as a family unit and increased bonds of love and loyalty in their faith community.

The most obvious difference is how the faith communities acted. For Angela and Becky, their church created a climate of guilt, denial and silence which created a theological justification for expelling Angela from her family and church. This led to family breakup and Becky needing to leave her church home. The lack of support meant that there was alienation from the faith community that has compounded an ongoing sense of grief and loss. For Sophie the story could not have been more different; the support, encouragement and openness allowed the family to survive and become stronger.

In Matthew 7.15–20 Jesus speaks about false prophets and says it is by their fruits that you will know them. It is hard not to see the outcomes of theological rigidity as bad fruit –alienation, pain and family breakup in Becky's story. It is equally hard not to see the actions of the Quaker community in which Sophie and David belonged as good fruit – wholeness, healing and grace.

Interviews from the partners
Relationships with the church

Both Rachel and Jim grew up in conservative churches but had already left them at the time of meeting their partners. Both partners already identified as part of the LGBT community themselves and met their partners in LGBT-friendly faith settings. Rachel met Ed through an LGBT Christian internet network that occasionally meets for worship, while Jim met Steve at a Christian event at university and then became part of the university chaplaincy community where they are studying.

In both cases Rachel and Jim met and created their relationships in LGBT-friendly faith spaces. This has meant that many of the issues of non-acceptance or difficulty have been avoided because they are not part of the Church where these difficulties are occurring. This has meant that their partner being trans has not been an issue in itself and this has allowed them to focus their energies on making adjustments to their relationships as the gender journeys of their partners unfold and they are able to support them through them. They are also able to draw support from their faith community. As Rachel comments about her church:

> That's been a great community for both of us... And it's been very supportive and lots of people wanting to just stand alongside myself and my boyfriend.

As both partners met via faith networks it has also meant that both partners see their relationships as bound up with their own faith journeys. This is particularly true of Jim who came to a university event as someone exploring faith and was at a Christian Union event where he met his future partner. Their friendship blossomed into romance and this has also coincided with a newfound faith that has been fostered and encouraged by Steve. In both cases the interlocking relationships with partner and church are as linked together as any other young couple who meet within a faith community context.

For Rachel it has been important to have rites of passage offered by the Church to them as a couple. She hasn't seen the naming ceremony they are preparing for at the time of interview as a private ceremony, but as a rite of passage for their relationship:

> One of the amazing things that is happening is that they've agreed to have a naming service and that is happening in four weeks' time... And I'm really excited and it's going to be an opportunity to just mark the moment... I guess not just invite God to make that connection and for there to be a blessing...
>
> I guess that's as much a thing for to do with God as well as the other people who are going to be there as well, myself included just to say...like all of this... This is who God has created Ed to be.

Jim was in the audience of a Trans Day of Remembrance service at which Steve spoke and was 'stupidly proud' of him:

> Steve did a speech at the trans day of remembrance and he said 'I want you to come with me'... And I wanted to be part of that...and he did this awesome speech...

Jim, who worships at an Anglican Church, is aware that there are problems for trans people and other sexual minorities. He realises that the Christian Union at his university know of Steve's transition and are far from happy about it:

> The physical change is more with him so people like the CU are picking up on it more...
>
> I don't know if he told you, but he had a run in with the CU. [They said] he should be happy with the way God made him originally, which made me very, very mad. But luckily Steve knew her and he said God loves gay, bi and trans people as well.

He is also aware that parts of the Anglican Church have very different viewpoints that have implications for their life together:

> There was the General Synod and the trans liturgy wasn't there and then there was the House of Idiots, I mean Bishops... It just 'goes' to show we are moving slowly...gradually tiptoeing... But hopefully by then, by then they may start to realise that God loves everyone, and God wants everyone to be part of heaven.

Who knows it's not my issue with God it's my issue with the Church and human self-centredness... That we are higher up than you and we can decide your happiness...

So it's definitely true that thousands of people have been affected by [the fact that] the trans liturgy hasn't been passed and it definitely upset both of us...definitely upset me, I really thought it would go through...

I mean if I were to go into the church that would be my thing fighting for equality, not just equality for trans people but everyone on the LGBT spectrum... Just proving that we can be LGBT and be in the church.

These thoughts, however, are removed from his experience in his own faith community, where he and his partner are an openly queer couple who are heavily involved in the life of their faith community.

Identity shift and adjustments

Both Ed and Steve are in the process of physical transition. This has created physical and emotional shifts in their relationships as Rachel relates:

We began to date and at that time it was a two girls' relationship. We then went on a break for things that were unrelated to any kind of gender identity and during that break last year he came out as trans. [I was] very supportive of that, in some ways I suspected that it might happen, and I think for me it's been... There's been moments when I think I have to adjust the way I think about things...

[Interviewer] **Can you tell me what sort of things?**
Things like...that are really simple like I'm not dating a woman any more, I am dating a guy now and sometimes wondering whether is there a loss... Is there a loss of that person I was initially attracted to? Is that person ever going to come back?That sort of thing.

...But some of things that have obviously shifted are the dynamics in the relationship and...

[Interviewer] **Tell me about it.**
Yeah so I guess...like the relationship is gendered in a different way now, and I guess part of that is...I want to affirm him in his masculinity and so the language that I use...and sort of the things you talk about

and the words you might use for it, beautiful becomes handsome, things like this... And being aware of that so there's those sorts of shifts that happen.

There are many insights revealed by this narrative. It has echoes from the parent interviews around the insecurity created when someone begins their gender journey and the sense of threat and potential loss this may bring up. Rachel openly wonders about the impact transition will have on the relationship and also has concerns over whether the trans person remains recognisably the person that is already loved.

There is also the sexual orientation of the partner. As the partner journeys from one gendered space to another, this raises questions about the sexual orientation of the partners. Rachel already identified as bisexual but also sensed a shift because she was now in a relationship with a man, where she had previously been in a relationship with a woman that had different gendered understandings.

Sexual orientation also came up with Jim whose previously relationships had been with male partners:

It's the fact that we're both part of the LGBT community and we're both...with myself...I have no idea what sexuality I am at the moment, but I feel that my mine is more internal whereas he is transitioning, it is more external, something that definitely people pick up on...

Both partners, Rachel and Jim, also bought up physical intimacy. Rachel touched on the observation that there were changes in their patterns of intimacy as they journeyed together:

Just kind of how we are when we are with each other, kind of how we are sort of like physically and that sort of stuff changes things... Yeah...

Jim also touches on the changes that will occur as the gender journey continues:

I don't really know what I mean...with trans people there is definitely like not associating yourself with your body at this point, so it is how we approach intimacy and stuff like that... That's been, it's been both ways how comfortable we are with each other, what we're comfortable doing...

> We joke about it quite a bit, he jokes when he goes on testosterone it is like a second puberty and his voice breaking and everything so I'd make sure I'd record him so I get all the embarrassing moments... We kind of make it a jokey thing but also there are serious moments when he says it's never going to happen.

These changes to identity are likely to bring up pastoral needs for partners of people on a gender journey as they navigate the physical, social and emotional changes that are likely to occur as their partner confirms their gender identity.

Care and concern

One of the overriding impressions from the interviews with partners was the love and concern that both partners had for their trans partner. They did not see their transition as a problem but rather as a source of inspiration. As Rachel relates:

> For me I'm...I've just been unspeakably proud and moved to watch Ed become Ed because...it's not only do I see him being so much more centred and settled [Laugh] in himself but there have been lots of things that he has been dealing with for a lot of his life...personal struggles...and since coming out so many of those things have just melted away... And it just goes to show the impact of trying to be someone you're not can have on you and the strain it can have on you in time. Like he's just the same person and he is more himself... This is, you're just you in full colour and 3D now...and you're so much more settled in yourself and see the positive impact it's having on you.
>
> I'm continually amazed by...awed and inspired by the courage of Ed and other trans people to be...to live as their authentic selves because in this world that is so, so hard. So I guess off of the back of that, whenever and if there have been moments when I've been like...I'm always reminded that it's, ultimately, it's harder for the person who is trans. It's hard to be trans and I think it's Important not to lose sight of the struggle and the difficulty your loved one is going through and how much of an impact it has if they know that they have in you someone who has their back because a lot of the world doesn't, and they need that place of refuge... Yeah, in a world that constantly undermines and is often violent to them.

This was also echoed by Jim:

> It is something that I feel honoured that he can trust me so much... I'm constantly happy to be there and I try to reassure him that it's going to take time... It's easy for me to say as I haven't been through it but I'm learning and it's new to me and I am there to support him in any way that I can. Taking things as they come...and help him along the way... to be there to support him in everything. And I made that clear and I love him regardless of where he is along the stage of transitioning. I'll love him now and I'll love him after...

In both cases the partners felt pride and awe in the strength of their partners' determination to become themselves. One of the insights from the interviews around pastoral care for the partners of trans people is that the partner may put their trans partner's needs before their own. There is a sense in the quote from Rachel that there are moments of frustration and tension as they continually navigate and renegotiate their relationship. While this is natural and normal, it is important that they recognise that each partner has their own needs that need to be fulfilled if they are to maintain a healthy relationship.

Concluding comments

What is striking about all these narratives is the part that faith communities can play in the lives of people impacted by a loved one's gender journey. In the cases of Sophie, Rachel and Jim they were able to find love, support and affirmation in communities that have held them, or are continuing to hold them, as they journey with someone through coming out as trans.

This contrasts sharply with Becky who has struggled without a supportive faith community [1] and as a result has experienced a far more difficult journey. So, what can we learn from these narratives?

---

1   She has since moved from her previous home and found a church that is actively supporting her and helping her. We hope that this community will be the type of faith community where she will be able to find a home similar to the other three interviewees.

The lessons gained from these narratives are that:

- It is important to embrace theological openness if you are a church wishing to become more trans-friendly. Churches must foster an environment where theology is openly discussed and debated. People in the congregation must be given the space to agree or disagree with any theological stance.

- Faith communities need to focus on supportive and loving behaviours and be prepared to support the entire family as they journey with their loved one.

- Attention to and care of siblings are a priority for the Church. If the parents need to be preoccupied with their trans child, the rest of the community can help ensure that the emotional and social needs of the other siblings are met.

- Partners may need to be encouraged to seek help, support and counselling to ensure that their own needs and concerns are explored and met.

- The support you need to offer must be multidimensional in that it needs to be:

  - theological – giving someone the tools to make sense of the gender journey

  - emotional – providing emotional support in a way that allows them to have a space to explore their own thoughts, feelings and doubts as they journey with their loved one

  - practical support in order to help when times are difficult, and this may include offering places for respite if the situation requires it.

- Rites of passage such as naming ceremonies are important. These are ceremonies that show affirmation for partners and families as well as the trans person.

Chapter 5

Towards a Transgender Inclusive Theology

The problem of non-inclusion

We have often heard from people who feel that working hard to include everyone takes a great deal of effort for very little reward. They point out that it also makes those already attending church uncomfortable and they may feel like they have lost what made their church special to them. While we can understand this sentiment, we believe that it doesn't appreciate that the effort used to meet, understand and make relationships with people different to ourselves can be beneficial to our own journey as Christians.

It isn't surprising that we consider our own situations normal. We tend to live, work, worship and socialise amongst people who are not too dissimilar from us (at least on the surface) and because of this the assumption is very rarely challenged. Often is it only through the media that we hear about people who are different from us.

Trans people are a case in point. Programmes focusing on surgical procedures and physical transformations may make interesting television, but it obscures the truth that the gender journey begins long before and continues long after any medical interventions have occurred. It also brings a false assumption that all gender nonconforming people seek to legally and physically transition. With little information we often rely on stereotypes. We talk 'about' people rather than 'with' them, so we often misunderstand and misinterpret their actions. We come to conclusions that are not supported by evidence. Sometimes we become fearful and/or morally superior. If we are trying to learn and grow as people and as Christians this is not behaviour that is helpful or productive.

Even when we are given information it does not mean it moves from received information to a change in attitude. I (Chris) remember many years ago when I was running a training course for a housing charity on LGBT inclusion. They had added the question 'Please state your sexual orientation as either gay, lesbian, bisexual or heterosexual' to the evaluation form. After sitting in his course all day, a confused woman came up at the end of the course with her form saying, 'I don't know what to put down I'm just normal.' After I discussed it with her she happily ticked the heterosexual box, oblivious to the sense of futility I felt about how little she had understood of what I had tried to teach her all day.

If we are part of the dominant group, we often gain little insight into the experiences of others, simply because we do not encounter them or have the opportunity to hear their different life experiences. Even if they are present, they are often not heard as they are not the dominant voice. It may even be that when we first hear about them they seem so different from us that we struggle to make sense of what they are telling us. We may feel uncomfortable and feel our own assumptions of normalcy are challenged.

Fear of the unknown and our unwillingness to examine our own opinions and change them is frequently behind the objections about making liturgy more inclusive. These objections indicate that people want to stay within their comfort zone. So what is wrong with this?

First, it can create a God who is white, male, cisgender, abled and heteronormative as our sole reference point for understanding God. This impoverishes our understanding of God who is described in many ways in the Bible, including as a shepherd (Psalms 95.7), a rock (Psalms 78.35), a housewife (Luke 15.8), an eagle (Deuteronomy 32.11), a mother hen (Matthew 23.37), fire (Hebrews 12.29), a freezing wind (Job 37.10) and water (Psalms 65.9).

New ways of seeing God also allow us new insights about the nature of God. For example, one of the more challenging images of God is one of the interpretations of the name of El Shaddai for God. While many biblical scholars interpret this name to mean God of the mountains, David Biale (1982) argues that this is not the best fit for the term. He argues that it is better interpreted as the breasted one or the suckling one. He argues that the name is not derived from the word *shadu* meaning mountain but rather the word *shadayim*, meaning breasts. He further argues that this name for God is often associated with fertility blessings in Genesis. For example, in Genesis 17 God introduces godself as El Shaddai and promises to increase Abram's descendants.

El Shaddai is also invoked in Genesis 28.3 when Issac blesses Jacob to acquire a wife and thereafter have children.

Seeing God in new ways can help us to understand more and more about God. The suckling, nurturing, multi-breasted Mother God who suckles her followers, provides comfort and is interested in fertility is a long way from the stern, angry patriarch, which is often how God is portrayed.

And even if we are incurious ourselves or reluctant to be challenged, we need to consider the price of our ignorance for others. In Mark 12 we are called to love our neighbours and we are told this is better than all the burnt offerings given in the temple. If we are trying to live a life pleasing to God, it is our duty to educate ourselves about others. It is not a liberal optional extra.

Other reasons for inclusion

We also firmly believe that faith should not only be advantageous to ourselves but also should help us to become more generous, open-minded and loving to all. This sometimes involves us stepping out of our comfort zones and learning and growing. We also believe that it is important to understand that a mature faith comes with fulfilling obligations to live a generous life.

Fairness as a biblical principle

The entire dramatic arc of the Old Testament can be interpreted as a story of liberation and seeking justice. The Exodus narratives detail a story of freedom from oppression to a march towards liberation. Deuteronomy talks specifically about the rights of widows and orphans eleven times. Both major and minor prophets criticise again and again those who deny justice to the widow, orphan and stranger.

The New Testament has similar sentiments. In Luke 16 we read the parable of the rich man and Lazarus where the rich man is punished in hell while the beggar takes his place among the angels and the patriarchs. The parable of the Good Samaritan criticises those who put their own personal purity and religiosity above helping people. The Epistle of James is highly critical of the rich.

It is difficult to argue that God is not interested in fairness. It is even harder to argue that it is not our duty to be fair. And we cannot be fair until we treat all people the same. Fairness means all being able to come to the table and see themselves represented there. It also means that sometimes we need to give a little more help and consideration in order to level the playing field.

Freeing ourselves from the need to censor and control so we can rediscover what church can be

Consider for a minute the amount of energy it needs to control people. First, you need to be able to formulate a set of rules and behaviours that must be followed. Then you need to find a way to teach your group of people how they should behave. Then you need to monitor them. You also need a way of catching transgressors. Finally, you need a way of communicating punishment to others to ensure that they do not follow the same wicked way. Quite frankly this is all exhausting. It takes time, effort, determination and energy to do this.

It also breeds hypocrisy. One of the sad stories of the past 40 years in Christianity is the rise of sexual scandals attached to the Church. No church has been untouched and traditions such as the Roman Catholic and the Anglican Churches have uncovered systems of abuse that have functioned alongside systems of censoring and controlling sexual minorities. Our priorities have not been sensible; instead of keeping vulnerable people safe we have been denouncing people who are not harmful at all. This misplaced energy has seriously eroded the ability of the Church to speak out on issues such as the growing inequality in most economies of the global north; it is hard to talk with moral authority about anything when you have been implicated in the systematic abuse of children and other vulnerable people.

Freeing ourselves from these systems and using the resources to equip people to be able to explore theology and come to moral judgements themselves would create more fully mature Christians and a more robust faith. It would also leave more energy for the work of Christ in the world.

Reimaging Church – everyone really is welcome

On just about every church sign there is a statement 'everyone is welcome'. In some cases, this is patently not true. There are many stories of people being asked to move out of 'someone's seat' or having many parts of the service where there are unexplained customs such as standing as the collection is bought up or the use of 'the grace'. These actions show who is in and who is out and are not welcoming to anyone new.

While on the surface we say people are welcomed we are really looking for more people like ourselves, or better still young families with children (until the children behave like children and are too noisy). When I (Chris) was planting a church in Birmingham in the early 2000s, I sent an email out to over 100 churches. In the email I said I was a gay man who was looking for a church to worship in. I received back deafening silence and three negative responses. One suggested they could overlook my sexuality if I kept quiet about it. Another confessed that her congregation was not mature enough to accept difference.

There is also a marked difference between toleration and celebration. In churches we often play down difference and encourage people to blend in. Subtle and not so subtle pressures are often placed on people to conform enough so they can be tolerated, and differences are ignored rather than explored. This is a form of invisibility that does little to change the image of the Church or to help us to grow. And a church that prizes conformity and lack of challenge is slowly dying. The 2016 British Social Attitudes survey observes:

> The fall in religious affiliation has been driven, at least in part, by young people. In 2016, seven in ten (71%) of young people aged 18–24 said they had no religion, up from 62% in 2015.

The survey is also clear on the causes for this decline. Roger Harding, Head of Public Attitudes at the National Centre for Social Research, said (2017):

> We know from the British Social Attitudes survey that religious people are becoming more socially liberal on issues like same sex relationships and abortion. With falling numbers some faith leaders might wonder whether they should be doing more to take their congregation's lead on adapting to how society is changing.

Given the continuing decline in religiosity in the UK, inclusion is not simply a nice thing to have. It is likely to become a survival strategy in the coming decades.

Liberation Theology

Having argued that the principles of inclusion are more than 'nice things to have' we need to have a way of doing theology that listens to those on the margins and critiques the ways that we insulate ourselves from those who are different.

We believe the most effective tool we can use to do this is Liberation Theology. The following section explains the history and concepts behind Liberation Theology and explores how we can use it as a tool to work out ways of worship that are welcoming to all.

What is Liberation Theology?

Liberation Theology started simultaneously in the civil rights movement and in Latin America in the 1960s. It begins from a fundamental biblical understanding that God has a preference for the poor, the powerless and those on the margins. It also understands that the pursuit of economic and social justice is a biblical principle to be followed. It is hard to ignore the very real concern that the Bible has about the oppression of the poor, and its critique of wealth and privilege. Liberation Theology also uses the life of the early Church (Acts 2.44–47; 4.32–37) as a template for how we should live. Early Christians lived communally and simply, selling what they had and sharing with each other.

The concerns of Liberation Theology

Liberation Theology provides a challenge to the Church in a very similar way as the prophets of the Old Testament challenged the established religion of their day. It seeks to challenge injustice and oppression and give worth and voice to those who are marginalised and oppressed by the systems and structures of empire in all its forms. Some of the specific concerns of Liberation Theology are as follows:

Poverty

Given its call for economic justice, it is not surprising that Liberation Theology is deeply concerned with the systems of economic oppression that hold some of the poorest in our society in places of poverty. As Christians we often seek to provide charity in order to alleviate suffering. But charity is always a band aid, because it does not change the situation that caused the problem in the first place. It also reinforces the status quo, because those who are powerful enough to provide charity decide what form it should take and who is worthy to receive it. The receiver must take what is given and how it is given.

Liberation Theology critiques the causes of poverty. It challenges the rich not to be charitable but to allow the poor economic justice. Unlike charity, economic justice challenges the rich to restore the rights of poor people that they have usurped and appropriated. Sharing is seen as restitution of those rights.

Privilege

The insidious reality of privilege is that, when we hold a privilege, we are often unaware of until it is brought to our attention. Indeed, we often see our privileges as rights until we are challenged. I (Chris) watched this in action as my own denomination, the United Reformed Church, painfully groped towards the affirmation of same-sex marriage.

I had been party to many of the conversations in URC churches and regional synods about the adoption of a principle to let individual church congregations decide to offer marriage to same-sex couples. I was also a voting member of the General Assembly that finally approved same-sex marriage in 2016. At all of these meetings many sentiments both for and against same-sex marriage were aired.

One of the major themes against same-sex marriage that emerged in all these meetings was that same-sex marriage somehow devalued heterosexual marriage. At the time this argument seemed illogical to me as nothing appeared to have been taken away. On reflection I realised that what people were saying was that they did feel a loss because their ability to see their own heteronormative relationship as morally superior or special would be taken away if the motion passed. Suddenly their relationships were equal to relationships that they considered sinful or misguided. What had seemed on the surface to be an extension of a right to others did in fact involve the loss of privilege for those who had seen their own privilege as an unquestioned right.

When we begin to include others that we have previously marginalised it can feel like a loss. When we begin to see other people at the table it may feel that we have lost something special that used to be our very own. We may have to do things differently because what has worked for us may not work for all people. While these are perfectly natural feelings, it is important to remember what we gain in terms of greater knowledge of God and others, and a sense that we are finding a maturity and tolerance that has previously eluded us.

It is also the right thing to do. We are called to be followers of a radical prophet who denounced religious privilege, included unlikely followers and reached out to those on the margins. If we call to mind the image of Jesus he is at the roadside healing, telling stories and preaching. He is not in a church surrounded by pious people. Why is it that we revere Jesus but then don't act like him?

Institutional power

Liberation Theology also criticises the systems and structures in place that maintain power and privilege. Those in social and economic power consciously and unconsciously create systems that make it harder to dislodge them from their places of privilege. Ways of doing things are configured so that they require insider knowledge to operate them fully. Positions are reserved for certain types of people, such as men. This is as true in churches as in our board rooms.

Liberation Theology critiques these mechanisms and calls for them to be changed. It seeks to identify the ways the privilege is maintained and calls for fairer, more inclusive ways of doing things that allow everyone equal access.

Justice

We often see justice as something that is dispensed that is closely allied to punishment of perpetrators. For example, when we speak about the justice system we are normally speaking about the arm of government that is about the apprehension, trial, punishment and incarceration of people who have broken the law.

This is a singularly narrow view of justice. There are several ways of looking at justice and punitive justice is only one. Johnstone (2014) also identifies the concepts of community justice and covenant justice. Both envision justice in a more holistic way with the emphasis on making things right and fostering peaceful and right relationships between people. To illustrate these types of justice he quotes from Desmond Tutu justifying the Truth and Reconciliation process in South Africa (Johnstone 2014, p.115):

...here the central concern is not about retribution or punishment but, in the spirit of ubuntu, the healing of breaches, the redressing of imbalances, the restoration of broken relationships....

This is a more helpful way of looking at justice. It recognises that being in relationship means that both parties have a mutual obligation to make the relationship work. When the relationship is somehow damaged, actions must be taken to restore the balance, so it can properly function again.

If we are all the children of a loving God, it is important that we treat each other in a way that honours our mutual obligations to each other. This means ensuring the restoration of rights to those who have been unfairly treated, ensuring that remedies are put in in place to prevent abuse continuing. As Evelyn Miranda-Feliciano (1999, pp.491f) notes, justice 'has a dynamic relational quality...any act within the covenant relationship that maintains, preserves or restores the foundation of a communal life is just'.

When we speak about justice it is important to speak about restoration rather than punishment. In being just to people who are different to ourselves we are seeking to create a relationship of mutuality and respect rather than punishment and censure.

Speaking truth to power

The Church has often found Liberation Theology difficult as it has held up a mirror that shows an image that the Church does not like. It threatens the way that the Church operates and questions the privilege that is embedded in many of the offices of the Church. Many Liberation Theologians have left the institutional church, often after many years of the Church attempting to have their voices silenced.

It is never easy to be told that you are doing things wrong, and it is particularly difficult in institutions that have come to believe that they authentically represent the voice and the will of God. It may be important to distinguish between worshipping an institution and worshipping God.

Much of the recent history of the Church has been an argument about where God speaks. Some people believe God has appointed people in positions of authority within the institutional church who are uniquely qualified to discern God's will. Others believe that the Spirit of

God dances in society and it is the duty of the Church to hear the voices from a wider humanity and respond to the collective voice of humanity.

Liberation Theology champions that collective voice. It attempts to articulate the concerns and insights from those who are not at the centre and calls for those concerns and insights to be acted upon.

Including sexual minorities and queer theologies as part of Liberation Theology

From the 1970s, theologians who were LGB developed Queer Liberation Theology. The first wave of this Liberation Theology began in a defensive way by challenging the traditional interpretations of Genesis 19; Leviticus 18; Romans 1.26–27; 1 Corinthians 6.9; 1 Timothy 1.10, all of which have been used to condemn LGB people. It also told the stories of faith and struggle of sexual minorities to stay within the Church despite the difficulties they encountered.

The second wave of Liberation Theology for sexual minorities has expanded from those traditionally condemned by the Church because of sexual orientation to include gender-variant people as well. It is often more assertive and seeks to create new ways of looking at the people that Church has often condemned.

Liberation Theology often uses experience as a starting point for doing theology (as we do in Chapter 3). In her work queer theologian Marcella Althaus-Reid (2000, p.126) makes clear the link between liberation theologies and what she terms sexual stories:

> The methodology of liberation should always be worked around elements of a passion arousing style. At a community level this has meant that people's starting point has always been their own experiences.

This ethos is also echoed in other writers:

> Once transgressive sexual stories are spoken, they become disruptive by challenging the status quo. They will be heard, interpreted, redefined and will present sexual possibilities. The telling of sexual stories is a continual process of 'coming out' revealing a (divine) revelation of sexual experience. (Simpson 2005, p.104)

The ecclesial considerations of homosexuality and other forms of non-normative relations of gender, sex and sexuality, provide an occasion, a moment of rupture, exposing philosophical and meta-physical assumptions that might otherwise be obscured. (Hutchins 2001, p.11)

If I'd known then what I know now would I have persisted in rekindling my love affair with the Church? But of course I would, it's my Church, my Virgin Mary, my Salve Regina as much as it is theirs. (Taylder 2009, p.77)

These sexual stories disrupt the ways we speak of both gender and human sexuality. They also attempt to give dignity and voice to folk who have found ways to survive, and even thrive, in environments that have been hostile to them.

If we seek to include people, we need to hear their voices, understand their needs and be ready to learn from them. This can be difficult and challenging for people who are used to speaking and being listened to.

Applying Liberation Theology to the way we worship
What is worship?

The Oxford English Dictionary defines worship as:

The feeling or expression of reverence and adoration for a deity e.g. 'worship of the Mother Goddess' 'ancestor worship' 1.1 Religious rites or ceremonies, constituting a formal expression of reverence for a deity. 'the church was opened for public worship'1.2 Great admiration or devotion shown towards a person or principle. E.g. 'the worship of celebrity and wealth'

If we take this definition as our starting point, we can see worship as our reverence and adoration for God that also exposes what we value. How we worship tells people not only who we worship but what we care about as a group of people. Visitors will be able to tell from what we do in worship what we believe is important and what we believe God values.

Therefore, it does matter what we say and how we say it in worship. It doesn't matter how many welcome signs we have, how trained our greeters, or how vibrant our worship, if we are not valuing the person who walks through the door. Consider this quote from Amos as a way of discerning how best to worship God:

> *I can't stand your religious meetings.*
>> *I'm fed up with your conferences and conventions.*
>
> *I want nothing to do with your religion projects,*
>> *your pretentious slogans and goals.*
>
> *I'm sick of your fund-raising schemes,*
>> *your public relations and image making.*
>
> *I've had all I can take of your noisy ego-music.*
>> *When was the last time you sang to me?*
>
> *Do you know what I want?*
>> *I want justice – oceans of it.*
>
> *I want fairness – rivers of it.*
>> *That's what I want. That's all I want.*

Amos 5.21–24[1]

Liberative principles to apply to worship
The Bible is not a weapon

I (Chris) believe one of the hallmarks of late 20th-century and early 21stcentury Christianity has been the defining of Christianity as being *against something* rather than *for something*. In this environment we have often used the Bible to justify our opposition. This has often meant quoting scripture out of context in order to denounce a group of people. In short, using the Bible as a weapon.

In *Transfaith* I (Chris) argue that the biblical objections to trans people tend to centre around the Genesis creation stories and Deuteronomy 22.5, which is about wearing opposite gender clothes. Even if this verse is taken literally, it would mean that those who identify as gender-variant could equally interpret this verse as an obligation to dress in ways that are congruent to their gender identity. We do not believe that the Genesis stories preclude the existence of gender-

---

1   See *The Message Bible:* www.biblestudytools.com/msg/amos/passage/?q=amos +5:18-27

variant people, they are merely silent on the matter and there is plenty of evidence of gender variance in other parts of the Bible.

Worship in which we quote the Bible selectively by picking out a verse out of context to suit our purposes devalues it. If we are truly seeking to understand scripture we need to consider when the verse was written, who wrote it and what people understood the verse to mean when it was written. It is only then that we apply it in ways that can help us understand how we should apply it in our lives today.

Spaces for listening rather than speaking

Our worship frequently has one dominant voice. It is often that of either the professional clergyperson or a worship leader who is deemed to be sufficiently trained to be able to impart wisdom. It may also be a worship band or choir with songs that speak of a specific type of experience of God and theology.

In either case there is normally a clear division between those who talk and those who listen. The audience may be able to join in with music or speak the words of the liturgy, but these words are not words of their choosing. This gives a very safe space for leaders, but a very monochrome experience in worship.

If we are to be challenged, we need to move beyond this dynamic. Bringing different voices to worship can be done in many ways. The use of readings, poetry or drama can add another voice to worship. Using film clips that allow people to hear from other people and other perspectives can also help people to humanise issues.

We can also encourage people to tell their stories as part of the liturgy. This may be done in ways such as people giving testimony or writing a prayer that is used in worship. A simple and effective way to do this is a 'songs of praise' type of service where people can pick their favourite hymn and explain why they love it by either writing or speaking as part of worship. The principle is simple: getting people to contribute something of themselves will ensure that they are not passive spectators but active participants.

Spaces to explore, learn and disagree

One of the dangers of passivity is that often a dominant viewpoint is presented in a way that does not allow others to disagree. Instead people sit in worship and are presented with the choice: 'believe this or you are wrong'.

We desperately need to teach people good disagreement in our churches. Often, we disagree badly saying things like 'I have a right to my opinion', which is only half the truth. The other half of the truth is that we have an obligation to be able to articulate and justify why we hold that opinion.

We also need to teach that we have the obligation to commit to careful thought and study. This means exploring all sides of an argument and forming our views based on what we have learned. It means reading things that we disagree with as well as things we agree with, in order to work out what we think. This is particularly important when we are holding opinions that do damage to other people.

Churches need to find spaces where people can do this either in worship itself or as part of our communal life. We need to emphasise that good opinions are thoughtful opinions that have come through mature reflection and that this is part of the hard work of discipleship. We need to be clear that simple knee-jerk reactions or lazy assumptions are not good discipleship and do little to help us grow as Christians.

Spaces to try new things and change our minds

Worship also needs to allow permission for people to change their mind as they acquire new experiences and information. In Chris's current pastorate he began talking to a very sceptical congregation about starting a meditation session weekly. They had visions of sitting in a darkened room with incense, sitting cross-legged, chanting Omm and being pressured to embrace pseudo-Westernised Buddhist new age hippiedom.

It was only when he began to speak about Lectio Divina, an ancient Christian practice that focuses on scripture or holy writings that he got one or two people to try it. Once they tried it they were able to speak about their experiences and encourage other people to try it. He now has a devoted group of people who need their weekly 'fix of calm' every Tuesday morning.

Within our churches we need to encourage people to be able to try new things and change their minds and see it as an outcome of growing and learning. Trying simple things like using gender-neutral pronouns in worship may seem odd at first, but it can help to explain that when we only see God in one way we are impoverishing ourselves and excluding others.

It is particularly important to talk about privilege. Once we are alerted to the fact that we are privileging one way of being, or one viewpoint, we need to be able to present changes not as impositions of 'political correctness gone mad', but as an opportunity to show the growth, maturity and confidence of a congregation that is able to change its mind to be more inclusive and justice-seeking.

Spaces to make amends

Many terrible things have been written and said about sexual minorities in the last years in religious spaces. There has been much discrimination and graceless behaviour. There have been many people who have painted themselves into theological corners and are still stubbornly sulking there.

One of the universal principles of Christianity is that there can be no forgiveness without contrition. While the Church has always done a great deal of good, it is not a perfect institution. Churches have made mistakes; they have been wrong about things and they have damaged people.

Our worship needs to reflect this understanding and act upon it. There is little use asking individuals to repent if we are not also doing so collectively. Repenting of sexism, homophobia, transphobia, biphobia, racism and religious intolerance needs to be articulated and bought to the attention of congregations. While we do not have to wear sackcloth and ashes all of the time, we need to face up to the fact that we have collectively not lived up to the biblical imperative for justice. We need to ask forgiveness and attempt to make amends.

Spaces to celebrate difference

Worship should also give people the opportunity to celebrate their own identities and concerns and events that are important to them. One of the easiest ways to do this is to celebrate days and festivals that are important to a community. It may be that you celebrate something that is important to someone in your church community. It may be a national day, a day celebrating an identity or a specific event in the life of someone, for example the 4th of July for Americans, Pride for the LGBTQ+ community or St Patrick's Day for the Irish.

When considering the gender-variant community, Pride or Trans Day of Remembrance are obvious examples of festivals to celebrate. This comes with a caveat. Over the past years we have told many people that they are not welcome in our churches and many have taken this message to heart. It may be that your offer to host a Trans Day of Remembrance, or a decision to actively welcome gender-variant people, may be met with polite indifference or even active suspicion. The response does not make the offer invalid – as the people who started the argument it is important for us to be the first to cease it and seek forgiveness even if it is not automatically forthcoming.

If you are hosting this type of celebration, it is also important to work with a community rather than attempt to speak for them. The easiest thing to do is to simply offer to host an event and meet with the people who are going to be involved and work out details together. It may be a healing activity for all involved and working on creating an event together allows mutually beneficial and healing relationships to form as a bridge between communities.

Liturgy with trans people

In addition to public worship, giving people the opportunity to mark key milestones within their own lives is important. Within the gender-variant community there are several events that people might want to mark.

Marking the change of name and confirmation of gender identity

This may be anything from a baptism to a change of name service. Depending on the tradition and understanding of baptism this may be the most appropriate way forward. Another way of marking this change could be a renaming service and/or affirmation of the beginning of a gender journey.

Preparation for treatment

For those who elect medical interventions a simple service to pray for healing may be appropriate.

Reaffirmation of vows

For couples who remain in relationship it may be appropriate to give them the opportunity to reaffirm their previous commitment and ask for a blessing on a new stage of their relationship.

Funeral

Where someone has died it may be important to mark the whole of someone's life including their gender journey.

It is important to remember that for some people these occasions may be appropriate and for others they may not. Some people may wish to celebrate these events while other people may wish to maintain their privacy. Not all gender-variant people have the same life experiences, and some may not need any celebration of any particular milestone. They equally may have requests not listed here. It is important not to assume but to ask what people would find helpful and work with them to be able to create an occasion that meets their needs.

Concluding comments

This chapter has tried to explain that the principles of fairness are not an additional 'optional extra', but should be embedded into our practice of identity as Christians. It is a message that can be difficult for people to hear as it often involves change, loss of privilege and risk.

Often we panic and attempt to throw the baby out with the bathwater, upending everything in our eagerness to put things right. After the dust settles, we grumble and gradually the old ways of doing things slowly reassert themselves.

The advice from this chapter is not to try everything at once. Do the things that make the most difference. Try to sing one hymn with inclusive language; try to invite an excluded group to use your space. Take little steps to show the roof doesn't fall in when there is change.

Also do intentional work with your congregation. Explain clearly why this matters and how fairness is not only a mutual obligation, but will also benefit them. And remember that people accept change at different rates. Don't race ahead with the few enthusiasts or stay behind waiting for everyone to catch up. Move with most of the people, listening carefully and trying to deal with any concerns as they arise. When people feel listened to and valued, they are more likely to accept change. Understand that change is often incremental and that it is only looking back after a period of time that you realise how much has changed. Be patient, as God is patient with yourself and others.

And again, be prepared to celebrate when things change. The first indication of a permanent change is when other people begin to see that this is their idea, and someone might even claim this was their idea all along. Pat yourself on the back if that happens and thank God that something you have worked hard for has been achieved.

Chapter 6

How to Be a Transgender Affirming Congregation

Outline

This is a practical chapter, linking the theology of the earlier chapters to the day-to-day realities of life in a worshipping community. Much of what we write here assumes that the trans person wishes to be open about their gender identity or gender history, but not all trans people do. Some will wish to be accepted by others, including their church, without anyone even suspecting they have undergone a gender transition.[1] Such acceptance would be far more valuable to them than someone commenting on their past while extending them a warm welcome.

'All are welcome'?

In this book we have used scripture and contemporary stories to outline a theology that is inclusive. As we've noted, one negative aspect of being human is to exclude others who do not appear to fit in with our own conceptions about gender, ethnicity or social class. Although as Christians we frequently recite the Creeds which affirm our belief in the Catholic Church (meaning that membership of Christ's Body is open to the whole of humanity), we are often partial and limited in our vision of what this actually means.

Many churches have caught the vision and express this in a sign outside their building or meeting place which boldly states, 'All are welcome.' Trans people and other minorities who experience stigma and discrimination are often sceptical of this sweeping claim. The fact

---

1   *Passing* is the technical, if slightly misleading, term for a trans person who blends in unobtrusively without disturbing gender norms.

is that trans people have not always been welcome in churches and are still not welcome in many.

This was particularly true 20 and more years ago, when the Sibyls[2] was formed, partly as refuge for transgender Christians who had been rejected by their churches. Today trans people are less likely to experience exclusion of this kind. Even so the 'welcome' for trans people can be conditional. Trans people can still be asked to step down from public roles (such as reading at services, leading intercessions, or participating in the music group) when they come out. They may be told to modify their appearance during their social transition. Alarmingly (since it contradicts the ethics of transgender people's care) ministers may even advise trans people not to transition, or if they have done so, to de-transition. Recent conservative Christian publications (Davie 2017; Roberts 2016/17; Walker 2017/2018; Yarhouse 2015) all take this line.

George, who grew up in a very conservative religious tradition:

> learned very quickly...the moment that I confided anything to a priest or a so-called spiritual person...that was a disaster. So I learned very quickly...to be very secretive... My mother used to name me the sphynx of Egypt so... It was life saving...

Maria approached her priest prior to undergoing gender confirmation surgery but the interview:

> wasn't a pleasant experience... He challenged me and said, 'If you were to go ahead and have this surgery you're talking about, what if I put it to you that that is a mutilation of your God-given body?'... And that still is what is widely believed the higher up you go in the Church, even Pope Francis, who does so much to make [the Church] more pastoral, caring and inclusive.

She experienced affirmation, however, from the congregation:

> The priests keep a distance but the people are fantastic.

---

2   http://sibyls.gndr.org.uk

What she found undermining was:

> This current of negativity...corrosive, I think, and prevents you from being fully comfortable with yourself.

Steve, a university student, felt that one campus Christian organisation 'weren't particularly nice' to him, telling him 'that it's wrong' to transition 'and so that completely put me off faith'. He had explained to one of the members that:

> God made me trans...to sort of help me recognise and really know my male identity.

but she:

> pretty much flipped it around on its head and said, 'Well God has given you this female body and maybe he has given these thoughts to test if you have faith in how he made you and he has given you these thoughts that you are male to really test that you are...you are female because this body is female', and I sort of thought...like, that took me by surprise and I thought about it a lot and the conclusion I have come to is that she was wrong and that God made me trans and transgender people are part of the natural variance of the human race.

The narrative Steve encountered, that being transgender is a temptation, because gender is inextricably tied to biology, was also experienced by Maria, who was about to transition when:

> a very close friend who was an evangelical charismatic Anglican priest...persuaded me that it would be wrong and completely ungodly, and I persuaded myself [of] that... To my great regret now that it took me another five or six years before I finally managed to do it.

Steve was more fortunate and soon discovered that the student chaplaincy:

> were a lot more welcoming and told me that you can be trans and Christian and from there my faith has developed and I got confirmed last Easter.

Some people turn to a virtual church because they have not been welcomed. Ed and his partner Rachel have joined such a church, as Rachel explains:

> both of us have been in a LGBT+ Christian community which runs mostly online through Facebook groups and is a support group for mostly 18–30s LGBT Christians and it exists...to be a safe place when someone is coming out and maybe doesn't have those kind of networks and that's been a great community for both of us... And it's been very supportive and lots of people wanting to just stand alongside myself and my boyfriend, so there's that...

For a church community to hold together a diversity of views around sexuality and gender can be considered a virtue, but Rachel said it was 'difficult to be there' in her former church which was 'still working out how they feel about gender and sexuality as a church'. This contrasted with the church they currently attended where the minister had 'agreed to have a naming service' for her partner.

> I appreciate that it's probably quite rare but it's things like that are what I'd like to see at the church in the future.

Given these contrasting examples of conditional and full welcome, how is the trans person to know, when a church claims to welcome 'all', that it really does mean all? How can they be sure, even before they attend a church service or event, that the community is living the inclusive message proclaimed in its publicity?

Flying the flag

One way to send a strong message of inclusion that LGBTI+ people are fully welcome in your church is to fly the rainbow flag[3] on the building or to add it to the church's website and literature. Knowing that trans people are frequently overlooked and can be especially stigmatised, even within the LGBTI+ coalition, churches sometimes display the

---

3   To address the specific needs of trans people of colour, some churches opt for the eight-stripe rainbow flag.

transgender flag as well.[4] This symbolism will leave the trans person in no doubt that your church is fully committed, not just to their welcome as church members, but to their affirmation as people with a particular identity and journey. As Steve observed, it helps:

> If they state very clearly on their website that they are accepting and affirming of LGBT people. Looking for the trans bit as well so it is all not assumed they accept people no matter their gender and their sexuality... And they have been quite upfront about it, I don't know, like open... A lot of places are but they don't say it and you only find out when you're in that community and you talk to people.

The proposal to fly or display the trans or rainbow flag is likely to provoke a discussion among church members about the nature of the Church and the hospitality of God. Some people will argue that it is unnecessary to be so overt: the ethos of the Church is one of welcome and there is no need to be specific, or one would have to fly flags for every other marginalised group as well. In reply one could point out that trans people, along with LGBI+ people, appear to face particular discrimination at the moment, and that the Church is one of the places where discrimination can be sharpest. Equality legislation has helped, but recent statistics show that LGBTI+ people still experience hostile social attitudes and behaviours that affect their mental health adversely (McNeil *et al.* 2012). Meanwhile, Church governing bodies continue to discuss, scrutinise and problematise their lives and loves as contrasted with those of cisgender people.

In other words, while there is still injustice to address, it may be necessary to fly the trans or rainbow flag, literally or metaphorically. As well as signifying a commitment to equality and justice, both of which are central to biblical accounts of the human person and human community, 'flying the flag' will also suggest the all-important quality of safety to the trans person. Here, without doubt, is a community where the trans person will know that they can be themselves. They won't have to hide their history unless they want to. They are not going to be judged or considered less than others. They will be able to participate

---

4   In addition to the rainbow flag, OneBodyOneFaith uses the transgender flag to signify that a church or gathering is a safe one for trans people: www.onebodyonefaith.org.uk/about-us/get-visible

fully in the life of the community according to their gifts. In a world where none of these things can be taken for granted, it will be a relief to the trans person to know that they are not going to be an 'issue' in this church community.

David, for example, considered it 'unlikely' that he:

> would attend a church that didn't have that as a prominent feature that's very much the reason I went to N because it's a church full of LGBT people.

Welcome, for him, meant that, though he didn't often come out to people:

> when I do, I feel welcomed when people are interested and when they reflect on that conversation...

Ed was also:

> at a point in my journey where I am only engaging with places that are LGBT affirming... I guess on a sexuality front that all sexualities are valid and also with gender identity that trans people are valid and we respect them and to celebrate that it is part of your God-given identity... Kind of I need affirming not just accepting.

He would establish this by:

> looking at the theology of the church around gender and sexuality.

This was equally significant for other participants:

> It's not a question of just welcoming me but crossing the gender boundaries and how the church copes with that. (Anne)

> Churches that don't make assumptions about gender...it's one of the most important things that I look for in any community. (David)

For Ed being welcomed meant moving beyond a generic 'welcome to all' to a specific acknowledgement and celebration of who they were as a person:

So it's not just like you're just like everyone else and we're not going to treat you differently sort of thing...which feels more like you're going to ignore this. I think it being acknowledged and, like, I guess some of the social struggles of being trans being acknowledged but also, like, my identity being celebrated...

Signing up for inclusion

If flying the flag seems too demonstrative for your church, an alternative is to invite your church council or trustees to sign up to one of the church equality networks. A body like Inclusive Church covers several equality strands – economic power, gender, mental health, physical ability, race or sexuality.[5] This comprehensive approach to inclusion may be helpful for those with reservations about highlighting welcome to a particular group, such as trans people (though the reasons for their hesitation might need probing). On the other hand, the specific needs of trans people can easily be lost in a generic approach to inclusion.

Joining the online directory of an organisation of this kind, so that your church's details are included on its website, means that trans people will know that your church is likely to be a safe space for them and how to find you. Choosing not to advertise your church and its inclusive ethos through this kind of network means that trans people in your area may not realise that your church exists and what kind of welcome it offers.

If there is a gender identity clinic locally you could make contact and advertise that your church is welcoming to trans people. Or you might want to network with a recent initiative, led by Dr Susannah Cornwall (forthcoming 2019) of Exeter University, to develop spiritual care for people undergoing gender transition in NHS gender identity clinics.[6]

Acknowledging the particular needs of trans people might also mean registering with an LGBTI+ affirming network, like OneBodyOneFaith, which is ecumenical, and has recently added gender identity to its existing focus on sexual orientation. Even if your church is thoroughly inclusive across the main equality strands, it could highlight that it is trans aware and welcoming by becoming a Visible Congregation of OneBodyOneFaith, or a similar organisation. Steve counted themselves

---

5   www.inclusive-church.org
6   https://humanities.exeter.ac.uk/theology/research/projects/transgender

'lucky to know people' in their city 'who can tell me where the trans-friendly churches are' but not everyone is so fortunate. Becoming a 'visible congregation' through an online network will leave trans seekers in no doubt that they will be fully welcome.

Joining a generic inclusive church organisation and/or an LGBTI+ Christian one means that your church can draw on the resources, like advice and training, offered by these para-church bodies. David, having described how a retired minister had come to a non-binary understanding of gender:

> 'What is this gender thing? I'm a man and I have nipples'...through reflection and study

recommended churches:

> having studies that will take you on the journey he went on...in a Bible study environment...you can explore ideas that they haven't talked about and they can be receptive...If people are stubborn, they are stubborn, but at least you can have the conversation... If the congregation is not receptive in the first place, you have to be more creative...but I think a willingness for the church leadership to think about it...

Anne agreed and planned to invite a nearby conservative church to join the congregation she belonged to when someone came 'to talk about inclusion'.

Churches that have successfully made this journey often go on to express their support for their trans and LGBTI+ members by participating in the many 'Christians at Pride' events which take place across the country. Steve was 'involved in having Christians walk' in their local Pride March. He also mentioned an LGBT+ specific Catholic Mass in his city, and the London one, at Farm Street, has a strong trans network. An increasing number of Church of England congregations host regular Open Table network services which are occasions for LGBTI+ parishioners and their allies to worship together.

Safeguarding and safety

Due to the mismanagement of historic cases of abuse by clergy and ministers, most churches and religious bodies have examined and improved their safeguarding training and procedures. The public review of past cases, like the 2018 Independent Inquiry into Child Sexual Abuse and the Church of England, revealed similar patterns between the way Church authorities have treated survivors of child sexual abuse, and the Church's corporate response to trans and LGBI+ people. Both groups have been held at arm's length. People's stories have been denied or ignored. The impression is given that it is somehow wrong or distasteful to talk about their lives and experience. Those who have perpetrated abuse against them have been believed or protected. There is also a growing awareness of the need to address the reality of spiritual abuse and its impact on people's lives, such as coercive or invasive 'teaching' or 'mentoring' that fails to respect a person's integrity and exploits their vulnerabilities.

The Church's reform of safeguarding generally needs to take account of the lack of safety trans people have experienced in our churches. Anne noted how trans people are being mistakenly regarded as a safeguarding risk:

> People today are so concerned about sexual abuse particularly male upon female...anyone who disrupts the traditional gender boundary for any purposes can be seen to be suspect and I think we need to recognise that.

David offered a more specific example, where their being trans was unexpectedly turned into a safeguarding matter. During their first year as an adult volunteer at a religious youth event:

> A girl told another person at the event that she thought she might be trans and she was only 14. The person came to me and said 'Will you have a conversation with her because, you know, you're trans.'

Wisely, David suggested they consult the coordinator, but the coordinator discussed the matter with the child protection officer and the outcome was:

> 'We don't think you can tell any of the young people that you are trans.'

The negative impact on David went deep:

> I never understood; it was a long time ago...I've thought a lot about it since. They were safeguarding the event and, in the end... Does that mean that you felt that you had to protect the event from me? Do you feel that you need to protect this young person or their parents or all of the young people from me? If I am a danger, why am I here?

He appreciated the organisers' concern about how the parents might react if their daughter returned home and said:

> 'I met a trans person and I'm trans and I'm gonna, you know, be someone else now, mum and dad, sorry...'

but questioned the underlying assumption that openly discussing the topic would have 'converted a nice normal child into a trans person'. Being trans isn't something one can 'catch' from another trans person, nor can one be 'cured' of being trans if that's what you are.

In recent years the UK's therapeutic bodies have reached a firm consensus that 'conversion therapy' or attempting to alter someone's sexual orientation and gender identity is both unethical and dangerous and should be banned. In July 2017, the Church of England's General Synod voted to support Version 1 of the Memorandum of Understanding, which related to sexual orientation. Version 2 of the Memorandum, launched a year later, includes gender identity as well.

The recent spate of conservative Evangelical books by Yarhouse (2015), Roberts (2016/17) Davie (2017) and Walker (2017/18) already cited, shows that church leaders are being encouraged, contrary to these Memoranda, and WPATH's Standards of Care, to advise trans people against transition, or to de-transition. Although offered within a framework of 'welcome', pastoral practice of this sort is both ill-informed and harmful. It is important that you are aware that this is happening, and know how to challenge it if it occurs in a church or network with which you are associated by contacting the local or national church safeguarding team.

A trans person coming to your church may be escaping from, and possibly even psychologically damaged by, this kind of approach as Ed recalls:

I was in quite a conservative evangelical church which I left and...I was really, really battling with everything, often having huge panic attacks about 'does God hate me?' I think meeting other people who are LGBT and Christian has been a huge help by squaring that up with my faith and that's been a kind of journey.

People like him will be seeking a community where they feel safe. They may need to talk through some of the harm that has been inflicted before they can begin to settle into life in a caring Christian community. Their safety, like that of every member of the congregation, should be paramount. The reality of psychological and spiritual abuse is increasingly recognised in the Church and should be reported. Even if the person in your congregation has withdrawn from that setting, the abuse may still be happening to someone else.

Pastoral care of trans people

The availability of confidential listening in a church setting can bring relief and be a source of hope and healing to those who access it. Ministers will have been trained in active listening skills and general principles of confidentiality, accountability and respect, but few will have a professional therapeutic qualification and affiliation. Most church-based 'listening' is precisely that and to describe it as 'counselling' is to suggest a professional skill and apparatus that does not apply in most cases.

When listening to a trans person in your congregation, or one who approaches you for help, it is best to acknowledge one's limitations and refer the person on to others if specialist care is required. This might be because the person's needs are highly trans-specific and beyond one's competence, or because mental health or other needs begin to surface for which specialist help is recommended.

Confidentiality (a key element of basic pastoral care in church settings) is likely to be high on the list for a trans person who approaches you for listening. They may wish you to know their history, while preferring not to share that information with other people in their circle, including members of the congregation. Betrayal of such a confidence would be a serious breach of trust and damaging to the pastoral relationship between minister and congregant. Some trans people will be understandably wary of their first pastoral encounter in a new setting, like George, who discovered that his supervisor 'was not able to keep his mouth shut'.

Knowing, from the start, that the trans person feels safe to disclose what they wish to share, while trusting you not to pass it on to others, is likely to determine their future relationship with you as the minister, and with the congregation. This is no different, of course, from any other pastoral encounter, but we mention it because the trans person may well be checking you out. Your church's website and literature are sending all the right signals, but the trans person may need convincing that these messages are real, and that they will find a welcome, rather than rejection. As Anne emphasised:

> the fear of rejection is one of the big things one is dealing with...and that is our fear...

Your reaction to their story will be critical to their sense of being either fully, or only partially, welcomed into the community. Your response will determine whether you are someone they can speak to, now and in the future, about their lives, gifts and hopes. Listening in pastoral care settings is nearly always a two-way street. Will you be open to learning from the person? Not just about what it is like for them to be trans or non-binary, but who they are as a person, and how their gifts might be harnessed in your church for the good of others. For too long the narrative has been that trans people are a problem for society, or the Church, instead of acknowledging (like other cultures have done and still do) that trans people bring something distinctive to a community.[7] For Sophie, being the parent of a trans son had been a source of spiritual growth and revelation:

> I have no doubt that God reveals Godself through these experiences and we need to heed them and celebrate them because of what they are teaching us about the nature of God and, if so, it is not about how we adjust to them or how we accommodate them but how...actually... is saying, wow we are being given something here and it's a gift.

---

7   Mollenkott (2009) identifies seven lessons that religious congregations can learn from trans people.

Role models

A trans enquirer might feel more at ease joining your congregation if it already has one or more trans members. If they can see a trans person 'up front' in worship, or in a leadership role, that will demonstrate that your church does not discriminate by keeping trans people 'out of sight'.

Ed lamented the invisibility of trans people when he was growing up:

> that would be really great in churches...to have trans role models because I think one of the things I had trouble with is not having any trans role models and never seeing any trans people when I was growing up... Then feeling like the only person in the world who is experiencing this and must be the weird one so I am just going to follow what everyone else is doing even if that feels uncomfortable to me. But having visible trans people that I could look up to...yeah, and have that represented and that people know that it exists and it's OK and valid...I think that would have helped me to say what I was feeling at a younger age and saved me feeling a bit of grief at it all, yeah...

This kind of visibility is relatively recent and although there are now more trans role models available, there may not be enough, as Maria has found:

> It puts a bit of a pressure on one to be a role model to always feel that when people meet one in church circles that they may not have met other trans people...I may be the only one that they've ever met...so they will base their views on me and that's OK. I have accepted that responsibility almost willingly...I believe that it is something that God wants me to do.

Being a Christian role model doesn't mean you'll always get it right. Trans people make mistakes, just like everyone else, but having someone openly trans in your congregation can be educational for other members.

Trans Christians find themselves modelling to their fellow Christians, in Maria's words:

> That it is possible to be...trans and...a decent holy Christian.

In various UK denominations there are a growing number of clergy (men and women), who are trans and open about their history. Twenty years ago, their existence was the subject of headlines. Today it is unremarkable; but here's a key test of how inclusive your church is of trans people. Would your church be happy to appoint a minister or vicar who had transitioned?

Trans Christian role models can be of help to trans people's loved ones, like Sophie, who was able to talk to an openly trans person with a senior national role in her faith community. Speaking with that person reassured her that her son's transition was perfectly appropriate and provided comfort and a sense of safety as well as *practical help*.

Making a meal of it

'Join us for the ladies' supper next Thursday.' 'The men's prayer breakfast is a week on Saturday.' Do such items appear on your church's weekly newssheet? Maybe you attend events of this kind. They're a popular format in some churches and can be very enjoyable. Binary trans people in the congregation can join the group they identify with, but might appreciate publicity that states that trans people are welcome. Ed explained how:

> There's often gendered activities that go on in church there may be a men's curry night or whatever... Churches seem to do these things... If the church is running something like that saying this is [for] self-identifying women or self-identifying men...would be helpful.

Non-binary people though might wonder why their church needs to divide on gendered lines like this, but as Ed noted, they can be included too:

> And maybe specify that this is open to non-binary people as well...kind of having that written in I guess.

The non-binary person's perspective is a reminder that the local congregation may need social spaces for those for whom segregating on the basis of gender, even for a meal, is going to feel strange and artificial. It also poses the question why members of the Body of Christ, in whom there is neither male nor female, arrange social gatherings based on gender.

One answer might be that, while Christ has broken down every barrier, including those affecting gender, social differences remain between men and women and that there is value, even in churches, of creating spaces exclusively for men and women. Unlike Orthodox Jewish worship in the synagogue, or Muslim prayer in the Mosque, very few Christian churches divide their worship spaces into male and female zones, but women can still be forbidden to enter holy places, as George, who is Greek Orthodox, explained:

> you can't complain, in the Catholic Church at least you will get nuns giving communion, OK? In the Greek Orthodox Church you will never get that. No. You are not supposed to go into the sacred part of the church, you are not allowed to step in if you are a woman...

Asked whether he, as a trans man, would be permitted to pass beyond the Iconastatis, or screen, into the sacred space of the church, he replied:

> If they don't know who I am 'yes', if they do 'no'.

He then added, playfully:

> I have sometimes been tempted to [make] a special visit at Mt Athos [an ancient monastic site where even female animals are not permitted]. Supposedly the only female is the Holy Mother, yeah...

Ed thought that theological language, as well as language generally, could be 'quite exclusionary to trans people', noting that 'essentialising certain body parts or qualities to certain genders can feel a bit alienating'; Marian theology, for example:

> Talking about pregnancy like this about Mary, kind of saying that about all women can be a difficult thing and...

Yet only modest adaptation was needed:

> ... it might seem a bit pedantic to say you could phrase things differently but it will make a big difference like saying you're welcome here and you are acknowledged.

Coming out as trans in a church congregation

So far we've assumed that someone who has transitioned has approached you with a view to joining the congregation or has turned up one Sunday. Another possible scenario is that you already have a trans person in your congregation, but they have not yet come out to anyone.

When you meet someone who has transitioned, their gender history may not be obvious to you and you know them only as they are now. When someone in the congregation comes out as trans, you and members of the congregation may have known them for months, even years, in their birth-assigned gender. This situation is more complex and requires sensitivity and skill on the part of the minister and congregation.

One possibility is that the person concerned may simply wish to inform you that they are trans and that they have no intention of transitioning at that point. They may be happy to manage their gender variance without changing their gender expression and simply need someone else to know.

They might decide to present according to their gender identity in certain social settings, but not all the time, because they are bigender (living sometimes as male and at others as female). Perhaps they have chosen not to transition due to family commitments or the possible impact on their job security. If they sometimes visit public spaces presenting according to their gender identity, they may wish you to be aware of that, as news of it could reach you from another source. Or it may be that the person is beginning to accept themselves as trans and needs time to consider the implications.

Each of these scenarios requires a different response and it is for you to supply the one that is most appropriate. It may have taken the individual many years and much heart-searching to reach the self-acceptance which has led them to come out as trans. If they are familiar with the rhetoric that denigrates and demonises trans people, they may need reassurance that their church community will continue to accept them.

Anne had received positive responses – people had said she was 'very brave to do this' and even if they didn't 'understand what it is' had promised, 'I will support you every inch of the way' – but she recognised that 'guilt is the real killer and that can be a real situation'. On the other hand, many young people have grown up knowing being trans is a normal human variation, in which case your encounter might focus on something other than their being trans. Jim conceptualised older and younger trans people by two historical phases:

> There's a first wave dealing with trans acceptance and they had to deal with a lot of shit...and it has hardened them and made them stand their ground. No less trouble finding themselves. But in the second wave there's been more time to find out who you are rather than fighting for who you are...

As we did in our workshops, you will probably meet trans people from different generations and their needs are likely to vary.

Leaving home: Trans Christians in exodus or exile

Sometimes a trans Christian decides not to come out in a community where they are well-known and moves to another church.

> Lucy [not her real name] had been heavily involved in her city church. She read the lesson at services, was a member of the PCC and a Deanery Synod representative. There were a number of churches in her neighbourhood, so when she transitioned she chose to leave her church and join another one which was, in fact, nearer to where she lived. She did not anticipate any problems transitioning at her former church, but thought that it might require energy, which she knew she would need to transition at work. To join another church, which she could attend as Lucy, might even provide her with the kind of supportive network that she felt she needed at this stage, and she was not disappointed. Within a very short time Lucy made friends with a woman of her own age and a younger woman with a baby daughter. They all lived near to one other, visited each other's homes and soon became firm friends. When Lucy fell ill and was dying, these women from her 'new' church were among the many friends who came to her assistance.

As this story illustrates, there should be no sense of shame or failure if a trans person chooses not to transition as a member of your congregation. Their departure need not reflect suspected incapacity within your church community to adjust to someone's transition. Like Lucy, the trans person may intuit that joining another congregation, where they are unknown, may prove better for them for any number of reasons. An obvious one is to avoid having to manage other people's reactions to their transition so as to focus their energy on the journey itself.

If the person is able to inform you before they leave so much the better, otherwise you will be left wondering whether you or the congregation had let them down. It would also be helpful if they were to keep in touch and let you know how they are getting on. Not everyone is able to do this, and some people prefer to make a 'clean break'. To picture the Christian life as a journey is a commonplace and trans Christian journeys often involve both 'exodus', moving on from one community to another, and a sense of 'exile' from people they have known and loved.

What will other people think?

That question is bound to have crossed the trans person's mind, and may well be crossing your mind, especially if someone says they plan to transition. What if their family and close friends are not accepting? It's not for you to take sides. By all means point the person and their loved one to sources of specialist help if they need it, including reconciliation services and support groups for families (see Appendix C). Your main role will be to ensure that the church community is one in which the trans person and their family continue to feel loved and held, as described in Chapter 4. Sometimes ministers provide the family support, as Anne explained:

> It was my wife who told the local vicar [that Anne was trans] and to know that my wife can go and freely talk to the vicar and indeed that the vicar gives the spouses support is an extremely important element...it is the ministers who have taken the initiative in saying to my wife 'Do you need help? Do you need support?' And they have been very good in that respect...

Transition can put strain on a marriage and some marriages do not survive, though many do. For a church to be home to people with conflicting needs can be testing, and you may want to identify an individual to befriend the trans person, and another to befriend their spouse, or refer them to a suitable spiritual director beyond the congregation. These family dynamics are another reason why the trans person might decide to move to another church at this point.

Knowing your congregation, you might be confident that most people will be able to adjust to the transition of someone they know well. Some may welcome it as a sign of the wideness of God's mercy expressed in their local church. You may be concerned that for others this looks like a 'step too far', though this could be a projection of your own anxieties about possible pitfalls. People's reactions are often surprising, and it is impossible to predict how anyone will react.

Should someone be condemning, what then? If you and your community are going to be true to the gospel of God's unconditional love, then you will want to stand by the trans person. Some of those who object may be prepared to stay and reflect on their own reactions. Others could opt to leave, as happened at St James and Emmanuel, Didsbury. There the church began to speak openly about LGBTI+ matters following the suicide of teenager member Lizzie Lowe, who had assumed she could not be both Christian and gay.[8] People leaving the church can be worrying, especially for small congregations, but other churches and members of the public will also hear about what is happening, and that may work in your favour. Some people will be attracted to your church because of its willingness to stand up for the vulnerable. Steve said that his ideal minister would be:

Willing to give trans people a voice where trans people don't have a voice... Willing to use their position to advocate for trans inclusion...

Gender transition and church management

When someone transitions in a UK workplace setting, various protocols apply. UK equality legislation ensures that trans people are protected from employment discrimination if they intend to, are undergoing, or have undergone, gender transition. Faith communities have negotiated exemptions to this legislation in cases where they are the direct employer, but churches seeking to include trans people will be guided by the legal provisions and good practice aimed at protecting the trans person at this vulnerable stage in their journey.

As a minister, body of elders or church council, you could be the employer of someone who transitions: the church administrator or a

---

8   www.youtube.com/watch?v=4Wz2ylsz9-I

youth leader, for example. In those cases the faith exemption is vaguer and depends upon someone's transition being seen as contrary to the 'firmly held religious beliefs' of a majority within a faith community. How one would determine that is unclear, but this clause appears to cast the trans person as a potential threat needing to be removed from their church role, rather than as a fellow human being and a child of God. Heavily influenced by a strand within religious culture that was hostile to trans people at the time the legislation was enacted – e.g. the Evangelical Alliance document *Transsexuality* (2000) – it is contrary to both the therapeutic consensus and the pastoral good practice we advocate.

Whatever the loopholes currently offered to faith communities by UK legislation, we assume that you would want to do everything you can to ensure that the trans person's transition in their workplace – in other words your church community – goes as smoothly as possible by following good practice guidelines. Responsibility for this will fall on the trans person's 'line manager', which could be the minister, church council or elders, depending on the church's structure. Following the initial disclosure of the intention to transition, the line manager(s) will want to work with the trans person to communicate this information to other employees (the church's paid staff), volunteers and users (for instance, the parents, if this were a children and youth worker) and agreeing a timetable for their transition in the workplace.

At this stage the line manager(s) may decide to seek external professional advice about workplace transition from an organisation like the Gender Identity Research and Education Society (GIRES) or Gendered Intelligence. Local circumstances will vary but where people are less familiar with trans people's lives and experience, a speaker from this kind of organisation can advise the leadership team on what to expect and how to avoid pitfalls. Often this is simply a matter of allaying people's anxieties, sharing good practice and ensuring that the trans person is supported and affirmed in their transition.

These measures are usually unnecessary when a member of the congregation is transitioning. Trans people's privacy has often been invaded by the media, especially during transition, so it helps if a congregation can simply allow the trans person to be themselves without too much discussion. Again, trans people's lives are frequently turned into the subject matter of debate, and the Church has encouraged this (for example, Chapter 7 of the Church of England's 2003 publication *Some Issues in Human Sexuality*). Trans people, however, are not a curious hot topic. Their lives and experience are not up for debate. An informed church will be able to create the climate of respect needed to keep communication open and address any difficulties.

Not in front of the children

Trans people frequently complain that they are asked to micro-manage their behaviour or appearance for the sake of other people. In the very first story in this book, Abi (who is bigender) was told by people in her congregation they would 'find it difficult' if she were to attend church as Abi. To protect themselves and their own possible reactions, they didn't want Abi to be herself in their presence. It was only with her vicar's support that she was able to worship as Abi and people have become accustomed to it.

Attempts at micro-managing trans people's lives can also be indirect. The notions that having a trans person in the congregation or that someone's transition might be 'confusing' for children and adolescents are common examples. This doesn't sound particularly welcoming, but rather as if the speaker preferred the person concerned to transition elsewhere. Underlying this can be assumptions that transition is unseemly or unholy for religious people, but as this is rarely directly expressed it is hard to engage with these mistaken concepts.

Overt comments, such as the suggestion that the existence of trans people in a congregation is a threat to children and young people should be robustly countered. Very young children may not even notice that someone transitioning looks 'different'. Older children may be aware and ask questions of their parents and church leaders. Some children and adolescents may question their gender identity as a normal part of their development, without themselves being transgender. This would happen irrespective of whether or not there was a trans person in the congregation, but the existence of such a person, who is affirmed and loved like everyone else, may enable them to talk through their own self-understanding.

A church that is unable to name and respect a transgender member could become a church where a trans child or youth begins to deny, repress or even hate themselves. The late Lizzie Lowe's story shows the tragic consequences that can follow when young people have to hide who they are ('Gender identity appears to be indelible from before birth': NHS 2008, p.13; see Roughgarden 2017), so having someone trans in your church is unlikely to destabilise children's sense of gender identity, but will signal that this is a caring environment to be in.

The arrival of a trans or non-binary person in your congregation, or a congregant's transition, might well open up a much-needed discussion about gender roles and expectations in your church. It could also be a lifeline to members of your congregation who have felt unable to talk openly about their experience. A visible trans person could be a catalyst to greater openness and the extension of pastoral care and support to others.

We know that transgender children and their parents can have an especially hard time. Schools, including church schools, promote excellence in this area by enabling children's social transition, including policies to prevent transphobic bullying,[9] but their parents can face hostile responses from other parents, family and their faith communities.

A widely publicised case arose in 2017 when Christian parents on the Isle of Wight removed the second of their two sons from a church school following the social transition of another pupil. They argued that the school's policy impinged on their and their children's belief that a biological boy cannot be a girl, but the media campaign meant that what in another school might have remained private became a public debate, adding further stress to the gender-variant child's parents.

Cases like this could give the impression that having a transgender child in one's congregation would be a headache, but most schools manage this scenario professionally, discreetly and without fuss. Churches should be no different and could usefully network with a local school that has successfully managed a child's social transition. If the parents of the gender-variant child need the church to make any adjustments they will tell you what they are, and if you or they need further help, Mermaids is an excellent resource (see Appendix C).

Toilets

'But which toilet will they use?' This question can arise in the workplace when someone is about to transition and the professional answer is, 'the one that corresponds to their gender identity'. Toilets are often the focus for a 'last ditch' attempt to undermine someone's transition.

---

9   For example, the 2nd edition of the guidance for Church of England schools, *Valuing All God's Children* (2017) addresses transphobic bullying.

We mentioned in Chapter 3 the so-called 'Bathroom Bills' in the US, aimed at forcing trans people to use the toilet that matches their birth-assigned gender, but which would be impractical to implement: in a society where gender-neutral clothing is the norm and many question gender stereotypes, ascertaining someone's birth gender isn't easy. Genuine concern about women's spaces being invaded by predatory men must not be confused with the well-established principle that trans people should use the toilet appropriate to their gender identity.

Anne thought that problems could arise when a trans person's gender expression did not appear to match their gender identity, citing a case where someone:

> insisted on using a female changing room in [a high street retail outlet] and that person was really making a point by quite deliberately challenging the gender boundaries...

Anne also noticed that in one public building they had visited:

> the disabled loos are very specifically labelled as trans-friendly – I don't know if that's positive or not.

David thought not, and that their primary purpose should take priority:

> Always good to keep disabled loos free for people who need them...

Toilets are one of the few gendered spaces in modern Western society, but gender-neutral toilets are increasingly the norm. As David observed:

> I don't see why they need to be gendered.

In many churches, unless the property is extensive, toilets tend to be for use by men, women and children, so the 'which toilet?' question is often irrelevant.

Related topics that occurred to David were night shelters, which churches often host, though in these circumstances:

> there is generally not enough space to segregate people you might want to segregate *anyway*...

Whereas 'overnight arrangements' for 'residential youth events' need:

> to be thought about with a lot of care and consultation with people who have thought about it more...

In both cases the overriding aim should be to signal that trans people can participate in the event.

> At this point in the journey with church and society with trans people it's nice if it's made very explicit, almost overdoing it, saying that of course trans people are welcome...

Rites of passage
Welcome/naming rite

Church ministers have been co-creating welcome or name change liturgies with trans parishioners for some time. Recently, the Church of England's House of Bishops decided not to explore a specific rite to mark someone's transition, recommending instead that clergy adapt the Affirmation of Baptismal Faith from *Common Worship*, and encouraging creativity when doing so. Whatever your church tradition, a trans person's request for a rite should be taken seriously and is an opportunity to produce a liturgy that meets their needs, while celebrating the good news of God's love in Jesus Christ.

Ed, whose own naming ceremony was just a month away at the time of interview, stressed that:

> the name change, and social gender change, is quite an important one...

and that this was not:

> dependent on medical transition because...it is good to acknowledge that not everyone wants that.

Worshipping in a tradition where he was free to co-create his own ceremony with the minister he still thought:

> it would be cool if the Church had something there as well...

Theologically the rite would be:

> the celebration of how great it is that you have found out what god wants you to be... You know that God has brought [it] about in you... I think...of the celebration of this as a positive thing.

He also recognised the need for 'flexibility' as 'not all people want to change their name', and recommended 'having a loose liturgy'.

Steve envisaged 'a transgender welcome liturgy' at 'the normal gathering of people...whether Eucharist or not' and at the point in the service where baptism might be celebrated. The service would signify 'official recognition' of the trans person's name and gender identity but should be strongly communal:

> a renewal of mission and sending out; a service that really affirms you are a church community and you have this person in your church community as well as a focus on celebrating everyone in that community no matter who they are, what they are doing or whatever journey they are on and just a really affirming service that reaffirms the sense of community...

Within this communal framework, which might include 'renewal of baptismal vows', 'our own specific liturgy' was also needed because 'you're welcoming...[the trans person] as they really are...'

Maria, who is Roman Catholic:

> would have loved a liturgy in my church a service of blessing to mark an incredibly significant stage in my life.

and found the lack of liturgical recognition in her tradition 'wrong and shameful'.

Recalling her own baptism as an infant she felt that she had been 'baptised as me' rather than as her birth gender, but would still have welcomed liturgical, 'acknowledgement...some blessing from God' to mark what for her had:

> felt like a rebirth into a new life I mean...getting rid of all your old clothes, some of that was very therapeutic for me... Changing all your documents... Getting a new birth certificate was incredibly moving, I wept when I saw my new birth certificate.

Becky saw the value of a ceremony for the loved ones of those who are trans:

> acknowledging there hasn't been a change, but there has been a change and just being able to mark that...

Supporting a transgender loved one could be '*tough*' so the liturgy should encompass:

> Reaching out to God for openness and courage for the journey, because it is a journey...

Biblical and theological themes

The Church of England's *Pastoral Guidance for Use in Conjunction with the Affirmation of Baptismal Faith in the Context of Gender Transition* (2018, p.3) references several biblical passages about new life and name change as well as recommending the use of oil. Our participants also highlighted relevant theological themes for liturgical celebrations with trans people.

Becky thought a liturgy would need to address the:

> theology of gender... You know God created good people in God's image both male and female, so God is not binary...

Rachel noted:

> there are so many stories in the Bible where people are given a new name... How have we missed this!

Matthew 7.18–20 also resonated for them:

> From a theological perspective it's...that bit in the New Testament when Jesus says that...you can tell if something is good or bad by the fruit it produces... And for me, I'm...I've just been unspeakably proud and moved to watch Ed become Ed.

Three biblical passages animated Steve:

One is one of Paul's letters where he is talking about living by the body or the spirit. [Galatians 5.16–25]

which illuminated his own experience:

Living by the spirit, which Paul is asking us to do, is really good, is to live as who I am, as my full self and then it is about the journey helping the body move towards the spirit, which is what transition is...

St Paul's description (Romans 7.15) of *'dealing with internal conflict'* was also helpful, as was the biblical compound *heneini*, meaning 'here I am' which was:

linked to journeying where we were meant to be... And the New Testament has lots of new beginnings in it.

For Maria too, St Paul had proved 'enormously helpful' despite getting 'a bad rap' for being a 'misogynist' but:

he was a towering spiritual genius...and I am always drawn back to the bit in Corinthians [2 Corinthians 12.1–10] where he talks about the danger of spiritual pride being taken up to heaven. God gives him the thorn in the flesh and tells them that God's grace is sufficient for him and God's grace works best in weakness and that's always spoken to me and helped me and inspired me more than anything else.

A Catholic, Maria was also inspired by Franciscan Richard Rohr's spirituality which:

challenges binary dualism ways of thinking. The way so many Christians are judgemental and narrow minded and excluding of other groups...

She believed that Rohr's teaching about overcoming of the *'egotistical self'* and cultivating of the *'true self'*, especially in *'the second half of life'*, held:

particular resonances for trans people and for me I have had to go through two stages of that..living in the true self I've had to get rid not just of my egotistical self but myself that was in the wrong gender...

John 11, as interpreted in US performance activist Peterson Toscano's poem (see Appendix D) brought healing and hope to Sophie as it:

> conveyed both the mystery and the glory of God's presence in all things. And that removing of the restrictions that we bind people in.

Transgender Day of Remembrance

Also known as the International Transgender Day of Remembrance, TDOR was founded in 1999 by Gwendolyn Ann Smith, and is an annual commemoration held on 20 November to remember those murdered because of their gender variance. Special services are held on this day and it is an opportunity for churches to be overt in their support of transgender people and to protest at the prejudice they experience. On TDOR 2018 the English Roman Catholic Bishops' Conference tweeted a reminder to pray for trans people. Mentioning trans people in the intercessions on TDOR is also a possibility, but as Steve said:

> Ideally, I'd want my minister to hold a service for that.

Other liturgies

Our previous book, *Transfaith* (2018), includes several liturgies to mark the various life events of trans people and their loved ones. They are intended only as a starting point and we encourage you to work with the people affected to develop your own worship resources for these occasions. Gaps remain, as Ed observed:

> The Church has generally not got their act together but for non-binary people...having nongendered liturgy for different things, including marriage, would be quite important...

The Sibyls proposed the idea of 'a liturgy for testing one's identity – the anointing of the undecided' and 'a rite of re-adoption of the parent or of affirmation of the family' when a parent or a child was trans.

If our cohort of participants is typical, you are likely to encounter some rich theological insights when engaging with trans Christians, with benefits for everyone in your congregation. Anne, for example, envisaged:

a general liturgy which is celebration of inclusion and welcome and love...which could be on a feast day of a church...something that moves things forward through a church or... an organisation.

Funerals

There are mourners who have attended the funeral of a transgender friend at which the person's transition was totally erased. The deceased was referred to by their pre-transition pronouns (*misgendered*) and by their pre-transition first or Christian name (*dead-named* – like misgendering this can also happen in life, sadly). For whatever reason, the family and next-of-kin were unable to accept their loved one's gender identity and acted as if their transition had never happened. These behaviours sound like compound grief: loss of the person the family had known pre-transition, and loss caused by their physical death.

Clergy and ministers, like funeral directors and crematorium staff, will sympathise with such families, while feeling uneasy at the prospect of a funeral that does not fully reflect the deceased and is actually contrary to their expressed wishes. Great sensitivity is required of the professionals involved but it may be impossible to persuade the family to acknowledge that their loved one was trans. Some families may even seek to exclude transgender friends from attending the funeral.

Ideally a trans person's funeral should focus on and celebrate the person they have become. A possible compromise, where relatives are unhappy about their loved one's transition, is for the funeral to reflect their life both pre- and post-transition. Recalling the height of the AIDS epidemic (when the deceased's sexual orientation and partner might go unacknowledged at their funeral and their gay friends be uninvited), members of the Sibyls suggested the option of holding a memorial service, in addition to the funeral. At such a service everyone would be welcome, and the person's life celebrated in its integrity and entirety. They also proposed holding 'two ceremonies, one for Mark, the other for Mary' if the person was bigender. One Sibyl, who lived sometimes as male, at other times as female, and who had been uncertain what her son made of this, was deeply touched when they were both discussing her funeral and he asked her how she would like to be dressed in her coffin. Helpful advice for trans people (including making a will, naming an executor, and writing a letter of wishes) to ensure that their gender is respected in death was produced by Morgan Potts of Gendered Intelligence and can be downloaded from the Corpse Project website.[10]

And finally...

In producing a book of this kind, we have listened to and analysed many spoken words, and read and produced numerous written words, but always with the hope and intention that words will take flesh in our readers' pastoral practice. The imperative of putting theology into practice was strongly affirmed by Steve:

> You can say all that you want that you accept trans people but if you really want to show trans people they are like affirmed and truly welcomed in your communities you have to do something. And you can't not do anything you have to translate it into action because I think one big thing that I've found reading the Bible and in church and stuff is that what it's about is having these beliefs but moving them and turning them into action.

If you have enjoyed reading our book, and its contents have resonated with you, we invite you to set about the simple changes that will ensure that your church is as trans-friendly as possible. Becoming a trans inclusive church is more than just 'a good thing to do'. It's a gospel imperative.

---

10   www.thecorpseproject.net/respecting-gender-death-advice-trans-community

A Suggested Outline[1] Syllabus for a Trans Awareness Day for a Clergy Continuing Ministerial Development/Continuing Professional Development Day

If you are interested in hosting an event like this, please contact the authors who can refer you to the skilled facilitation needed for this kind of programme.

The pastoral cycle

- Experience – medical issues; interflow between emotions; spirituality; coming out whole.

Scripture

- Take the Bible verses head on – deal with mechanistic, literalistic interpretations of Genesis on male and female.

- Ministers rarely address Genesis or admit that it is not a science text book.

Pastoral care basics

- Process of transition – stresses people go through.

---

1   With our thanks to the Sibyls for brainstorming this list.

- You shouldn't quiz church attenders about their gender history – let them tell you.

- Don't react inappropriately to someone who doesn't conform to gender norms.

- Use of trans role models within the church congregation.

- The trans person to do the training – important that the ministers actually meet trans people as part of the training.

- The Sibyls as a potential training resource.

- Pastoral care – churches differ as do trans people, e.g. a mid-life transition is different from that of a younger person; the different size of churches – these differences could be addressed via group work.

- Use the Genderbread Person diagram (see Appendix B) which promotes clarity and understanding about the differences between sex/sexual, orientation/gender, identity/gender expression.

- Addressing the misconception that the motivation is sexual.

The Genderbread Person

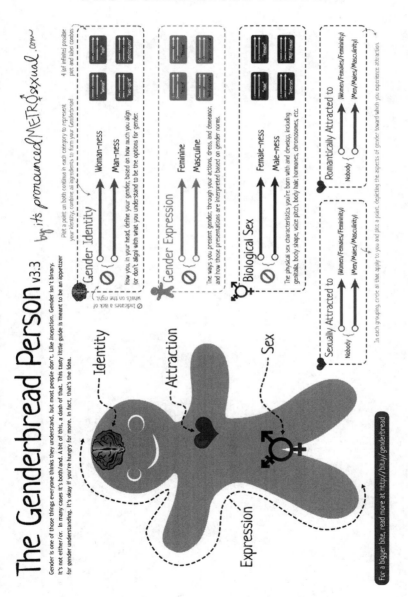

The Genderbread Person v3.3

by *it's pronounced* METROSexual.com

Gender is one of those things everyone thinks they understand, but most people don't. Like inception. Gender isn't binary. It's not either/or. In many cases it's both/and. A bit of this, a dash of that. This tasty little guide is meant to be an appetizer for gender understanding. It's okay if you're hungry for more. In fact, that's the idea.

⊘ indicates a lack of what's on the right.

Gender Identity

Woman-ness
Man-ness

How you, in your head, define your gender, based on how much you align (or don't align) with what you understand to be the options for gender.

Gender Expression

Feminine
Masculine

The ways you present gender; through your actions, dress, and demeanor, and how those presentations are interpreted based on gender norms.

Biological Sex

Female-ness
Male-ness

The physical sex characteristics you're born with and develop, including genitalia, body shape, voice pitch, body hair, hormones, chromosomes, etc.

Plot a point on both continua in each category to represent your identity, combine all ingredients to form your Genderbread
4 (of infinite) possible plot and label combos.

Sexually Attracted to

Nobody
(Women/Females/Femininity)
(Men/Males/Masculinity)

Romantically Attracted to

Nobody
(Women/Females/Femininity)
(Men/Males/Masculinity)

In each grouping, circle all that apply to you and plot a point, depicting the aspects of gender toward which you experience attraction.

— Identity

— Attraction

— Sex

Expression

For a bigger bite, read more at http://bit.ly/genderbread

157

Useful Organisations and Networks

Christian and trans

The Sibyls – a UK-based confidential Christian spirituality group for trans people, their partners and supporters. http://sibyls.gndr.org.uk

LGTBI+ Christian organisations that support trans people

Accepting Evangelicals – www.acceptingevangelicals.org/transgender

Beacon – United Reformed Church LGBT+ network. https://beaconurc.org

Christians at Pride – www.christiansatpride.com

Diverse Church – caters for LGBT Christian youth (18–30 years). https://diversechurch.website Diverse Church's website also has a useful Trans Theology 101:

> https://diversechurch.website/home/trans-theology-101-the-very-basics

European Forum of LGBT Christian Groups – The Euro-Forum holds an annual conference in a European city, preceded by three pre-conferences – for men, for women and for trans people. www.euroforumlgbtchristians.eu

Gathering Voices – 'An ongoing series of events, conferences and resources aimed at enabling churches to move from welcome to full inclusion of everyone.'

> https://gatheringvoices.info/about-gattering-voices

LGBT Catholics Westminster – welcomes LGBT Catholics, parents, parents, families and friends to Masses held on the 2nd and 4th Sundays of each month at a London Catholic church. https://sites.google.com/site/lgbtcw/news-notes

Open Table network – ecumenical Christian worshipping communities meeting in different venues across England and Wales offering 'Safe, sacred space for LGBTQIA+ Christians'.

http://opentable.lgbt

Church organisations that promote full inclusion

Inclusive Church – a network of churches, groups and individuals with a shared vision: a church which does not discriminate on the grounds of economic power, gender, mental health, physical ability, race or sexuality. To join Inclusive Church:

www.inclusive-church.org/join-inclusive-church

OneBodyOneFaith (OBOF) – an ecumenical organisation campaigning for full LGBTI+ inclusion and affirmation within the life of the Church. OBOF has recently extended its reach to include gender-variant people, and information about how to become one of OBOF's Visible Congregations, including specifically supporting trans people, can be found here:

www.onebodyonefaith.org.uk/about-us/get-visible/welcoming-congregations

The Ozanne Foundation – believes in a world where all are accepted and equally valued. We therefore work with religious organisations around the world to eliminate discrimination based on sexuality or gender in order to celebrate the equality and diversity of all.

https://ozanne.foundation

Organisations that offer information and advice to trans people and their loved ones

Depend – support for UK adults with a trans partner, friend and adult family member.

www.depend.org.uk

Gendered Intelligence – specialises in supporting trans people under the age of 21, their parents and carers; provides trans youth programmes and trans awareness training for all sectors, including schools.

www.genderedintelligence.co.uk

Gender Identity Research & Education Society (GIRES) – aims to improve the lives of trans and gender nonconforming people of all ages by working with them, drawing on the latest scientific research, and delivering training to public and private sector organisations.

www.gires.org.uk

Mermaids – the main UK organisation supporting gender nonconforming children, young people and their families, it also provides resources for schools and public bodies.

www.mermaidsuk.org.uk/about-mermaids.html

Grave Robbers by Peterson Toscano

Lazarus, came forth, gleaming white,
A pillar wrapped tight outside his tomb.
Jesus looked at us, 'Take off the grave clothes,
And let him go.'

Panic twisted my gut like a wet washrag
Wringing out courage.

Who knows how to undress a mummy raised from the dead?
Does one start at the heart or close to the head?
We circled him as if he were a bomb to diffuse.
Then we began in earnest,
Unwinding, tearing, speaking comfort as we went.
The crowd pressed in hurling advice like stones.

Lazarus stood like marble, cold from his grave,
While we sweated in the cruel sun,
Unwrapping his trappings.
But suddenly, (or did it take years?)
It was complete.
Mary and Martha washed their brother in tears:

He was free – naked and in his right mind.

References

Althaus-Reid, M. (2000) *Indecent Theology*. London: Routledge.

Archbishops' Council (2003) *Some Issues in Human Sexuality: A Guide to the Debate*. London: Church House Publishing.

Ballard, P. and Pritchard, J. (2006, first published 1996) *Practical Theology in Action: Christian Thinking in the Service of Church and Society*. London: SPCK.

Beardsley, C. (2005) 'Taking issue: The transsexual hiatus in *Some Issues in Human Sexuality*.' *Theology 58*, 845, 338–346.

Beardsley, C. and O'Brien, M. (2000, 2004, 2007) 'The Transsexual Person Is My Neighbour: Pastoral Guidelines for Christian Clergy, Pastors and Congregations, Brighton: Gender Trust.' Available at http://sibyls.gndr.org.uk/documents/SuA0110c%20The%20Transexual%20Person%20is%20my%20Neighbour%202007.pdf, accessed on 28 July 2019.

Beardsley, C. and O'Brien, M. (eds) (2016) *This Is My Body: Hearing the Theology of Transgender People*. London: Darton, Longman & Todd.

Biale, D. (1982) 'The God with breasts: El Shaddai in the Bible.' *History of Religions 21*, 3, 240–256.

Bischoff, G., Warnaar, B., Barajas, M. and Harkiran, D. (2011) 'Thematic analysis of the experiences of wives who stay with husbands who transition male-to-female.' *Michigan Family Review 15*, 1, 16–34.

Bockting, W.O., Knudson G. and Goldberg, J. (2006) 'Counselling and mental health care for transgender adults and loved ones.' *International Journal of Transgenderism 9*, 3–4, 35–82.

Brooker, W. (2017) *Forever Stardust: David Bowie Across the Universe*. London & New York: I.B. Tauris.

Brown, G. (1966) *I Want What I Want*. London: Weidenfeld & Nicholson.

Brown, G. (2006) 'Transsexuals in the Military: Flight into Hyper Masculinity.' In S. Stryker and S. Whittle (eds) *The Transgender Studies Reader*. New York: Routledge.

Bruce, F.F. (1982) *The Epistle to the Galatians: A Commentary on the Greek Text*. Exeter: The Paternoster Press.

Burns, C. (ed.) (2018) *Trans Britain: Our Journey from the Shadows*. London: Unbound.

Butler, J. (2006, first published 1990) *Gender Trouble: Feminism and the Subversion of Identity. With an introduction by the author.* New York & London: Routledge Classics.

Camosy, C.C. (2018) 'Ethicist says Church teaching on gender "not incompatible" with accepting trans identity.' Available at https://cruxnow.com/interviews/2018/07/26/ethicist-says-church-teaching-on-gender-not-incompatible-with-accepting-trans-identity, accessed on 28 November 2018.

Chase, L. (2011) 'Wives' tales: The experience of Trans partners.' *Journal of Gay and Lesbian Social Services 23*, 4, 429–451.

Church of England (2017) Valuing All God's Children. 2nd edition. Available at https://www.churchofengland.org/sites/default/files/2019-07/Valuing%20All%20God%27s%20Children%20July%202019_0.pdf, accessed on 14 January 2019.

Church of England (2018) Pastoral Guidance for Use in Conjunction with the Affirmation of Baptismal Faith in the Context of Gender Transition. Available at https://www.churchofengland.org/sites/default/files/2019-06/Pastoral%20Guidance-Affirmation-Baptismal-Faith-Context-Gender-Transition.pdf, accessed on 14 January 2019.

Conroy, M. (2010) 'Treating transgendered children: Clinical methods and religious mythology.' *Zygon 45*, 2, 301–316.

Cornwall, S. (2010) *Sex and Uncertainty in the Body of Christ: Intersex Conditions and Christian Theology.* London & Oakville, CT: Equinox.

Cornwall, S. (forthcoming 2019) 'Healthcare chaplaincy and spiritual care for trans people: Envisaging the future.' *Health and Social Care Chaplaincy.*

Cowell, R. (1954) *An Autobiography: Roberta Cowell's Story.* New York: British Book Centre. Available at www.transviden.dk/artikler/Roberta-Cowells-Story.pdf, accessed on 28 July 2019.

Cupitt, D. (1995, first published 1991) *What Is a Story?* London: SCM.

Danvers Statement on Biblical Manhood and Womanhood (published 1998) Available at https://cbmw.org/uncategorized/the-danvers-statement, accessed on 29 July 2019.

Davie, M. (2017) *Transgender Liturgies: Should the Church of England Develop Liturgical Materials to Mark Gender Transition?* London: The Latimer Trust.

DeFranza, M.K. (2015) *Sex Difference in Christian Theology: Male, Female, and Intersex in the Image of God.* Grand Rapids, MI, Cambridge UK: Eerdmans.

Dietert, M. and Dentice, D. (2013) 'Growing up trans: Socialization and the gender binary.' *Journal of GLBT Family Studies 9*, 1, 24–42.

Dillon, M./Jivaka, L. (2017) *Out of the Ordinary: A Life of Gender and Spiritual Transitions.* New York: Fordham University Press.

Dowd, C. and Beardsley C. with J. Tanis (2018) *Transfaith: A Transgender Pastoral Resource*. London: Darton, Longman & Todd.

Drury, J. (1973) *Luke*. London & Glasgow: Collins.

Evangelical Alliance (2000) *Transsexuality*. London: Paternoster Press.

Fonrobert, C.E. (n.d) 'Gender identity in Halakhic discource.' Available at https://jwa.org/encyclopedia/article/gender-identity-in-halakhic-discourse, accessed on 22 July 2019.

Forcier, M. and Johnson, M. (2013) 'Screening, identification, and support of gender non-conforming children and families.' *Journal of Paediatric Nursing 28*, 1, 100–102.

Ford, C. (2018) 'Transgender bodies, Catholic schools and a queer Natural Law theology of exploration.' *The Journal of Moral Theology 7*, 1, 70–98.

Futty, J. (2010) 'Challenges posed by transgender-passing within ambiguities and interrelations.' *Graduate Journal of Social Science 7*, 2, 57–75.

Gill, S. (2009) 'Christian Manliness Unmanned: Masculinity and Religion in Nineteenth- and Twentieth-Century Western Society.' In B. Krondorfer (ed.) *Men and Masculinities in Christianity and Judaism: A Critical Reader.* London: SCM.

Grossman, A. and. D'Augelli, A. (2006) 'Transgender youth: Invisible and vulnerable.' *Journal of Homosexuality 51*, 1, 111–128.

Guest, D. (2006) 'Deuteronomy.' In D. Guest, R.E. Goss, M. West and T. Bohache (eds) *Queer Bible Commentary*. London: SCM Press.

Harding, R. (2017) British Social Attitudes: Record Number of Brits with No Religion. Available at www.natcen.ac.uk/news-media/press-releases/2017/september/british-social-attitudes-record-number-of-brits-with-no-religion, accessed on 26 September 2019.

Hartke, A. (2018) *Transforming: The Bible and the Lives of Transgender Christians*. Louisville, KT: John Knox Press.

Herzer, L. (2016) *The Bible and the Transgender Experience: How Scripture Supports Gender Variance*. Cleveland, OH: The Pilgrim Press.

Hirschfeld, M. (1991, first published 1910) *Transvestites: The Erotic Desire to Cross-dress*. Amherst, NY: Prometheus Books.

HM Government (2018) *National LGBT Survey Research Report*. Available at www.gov.uk/government/publications/national-lgbt-survey-summary-report, accessed on 29 July 2019.

Holland, J. and Henriot, P. (1983, first published 1980) *Social Analysis: Linking Faith and Justice*. Revised and enlarged edition. Washington DC: Dove Communications & Orbis Books in collaboration with the Center of Concern.

Johnstone, G. (2014) 'Towards a "justice agenda" for restorative justice.' *Restorative Justice 2*, 2, 115–123.

Hutchins, C.K. (2001) 'Holy ferment: Queer philosophical destabilizations and the discourse on lesbian, gay, bisexual and transgender lives in Christian institutions.' *Theology & Sexuality 8*, 15, 9–22.

Kennedy, N. and Hellen, M. (2010) 'Transgender children: More than a theoretical challenge.' *Graduate Journal of Social Science 7*, 2, 25–43.

Kolakowski, V.S. (1997a) 'The concubine and the eunuch. Queering up the breeder's Bible.' In R. Goss and A.A.S. Strongheart (eds) *Our Family, Our Values*. New York: Haworth Press.

Kolakowski, V.S. (1997b) 'Towards a Christian ethical response to transsexual persons.' *Theology and Sexuality 3*, 6, 10–31.

Kolakowski, V.S. (2000) 'Throwing a party. Patriarchy, gender and the death of Jezebel.' In R. Goss and M. West (eds) *Take Back the Word: A Queer Reading of the Bible*. Cleveland, OH: Pilgrim Press.

McFadyen, A.I. (1990) *The Call to Personhood: A Christian Theory of the Individual in Social Relationships*. Cambridge: Cambridge University Press.

McNeil, J., Bailey, L., Ellis, S., Morton, J. and Regan, M. (2012) *Trans Mental Health and Emotional Wellbeing Study*. Scottish Transgender Alliance, Trans Resource and Empowerment Centre, TransBareAll, Traverse Research, Sheffield Hallam University.

Marks, J. (2009, first published 2008) *Exchanging the Truth of God for a Lie: One Man's Spiritual Journey to Find the Truth about Homosexuality and Same-Sex Partnerships,* 2nd edn. Courage UK.

Memorandum of Understanding on Conversion Therapy, Version 2 (2017) Available at https://www.psychotherapy.org.uk/wp-content/uploads/2017/10/UKCP-Memorandum-of-Understanding-on-Conversion-Therapy-in-the-UK.pdf, accessed on 29 July 2019.

Miranda-Feliciano, E. (1999). In D. Alexander and P. Alexander *The New Lion Handbook to the Bible* 491ff. Oxford: Lion.

Mollenkott, V.R. (2001) *Omnigender: A Trans-Religious Approach*. Cleveland, OH: The Pilgrim Press.

Mollenkott, V.R. (2009) 'We Come Bearing Gifts: Seven Lessons Religious Congregations Can Learn From Transpeople' (sic). In M. Althaus-Reid and L. Isherwood (eds) *Trans/formations*. London: SCM.

Mollenkott, V.R. and Sheridan, V. (2003) *Transgender Journeys*. Eugene, OR: Resource Publications.

Morrison, E.G. (2010) 'Transgender as ingroup or outgroup? Lesbian, gay, and bisexual viewers respond to a transgender character in daytime television.' *Journal of Homosexuality 57*, 5, 650–665.

The Nashville Statement (2017) Available at https://cbmw.org/nashville-statement, accessed on 29 July 2019.

NHS (2008) *Medical Care for Gender-Variant Children and Young People: Answering Families' Questions*. Available at https://transfigurations.org.uk/filestore/Medical_care_for_gender_variant_children.pdf, accessed on 29 July 2019.

Nodin, N., Peel, E., Tyler, A., and Rivers, I. (2015) *The RaRE Research Report: LGB&T Mental Health – Risk and Resilience Explored*. London: PACE.

Norwood, K. (2012) 'Transitioning meanings? Family members' communicative struggles surrounding transgender identity.' *Journal of Family Communication 12*, 1, 75–92.

O'Donovan, O. (1982) *Transsexualism and Christian Marriage*. Bramcote: Grove Books.

Potts, M. (2016) 'Ensure your gender is respected and your wishes carried out after your death. Information for trans people in England and Wales.' Corpse Project & Gendered Intelligence. Available at www.thecorpseproject.net/respecting-gender-death-advice-trans-community, accessed on 15 January 2019.

Raymond, J. (1979) *The Transsexual Empire*. Boston, MA: Beacon Press.

Reay L. (2009) 'Towards a transgender theology: Que(e)rying the eunuchs.' In M. Althaus-Reid and L. Isherwood (eds) *Trans/Formations*. London: SCM.

Rees, M. (2009, first published 1996) *Dear Sir or Madam: A Journey from Female to Male*. Tunbridge Wells: Mallard.

Roberts, V. (2016/17) *Transgender*. Epsom: The Good Book Company.

Roth, U. (2014) Source: Zeitschrift für die neutestamentliche Wissenschaft und die Kunde der älteren Kirche 105, 1, 102–130.

Roughgarden, J. (2017) 'Homosexuality and Evolution: A Critical Appraisal.' In M. Tibayrenc and F.J. Ayala (eds) *On Human Nature: Biology, Psychology, Ethics, Politics, and Religion*. London, San Diego, CA, Cambridge, MA, and Oxford: Academic Press.

Schüssler Fiorenza, E. (1994, first published 1983) *In Memory of Her: A Feminist Theological Reconstruction of Christian Origins,* 2nd edition. London: SCM.

Shaw, J. (2015/2017) 'Conflicts Within the Anglican Communion.' In A. Thatcher (ed.) *The Oxford Handbook of Theology, Sexuality and Gender*. Oxford: Oxford University Press.

Sheridan V. (2001) *Crossing Over: Liberating the Transgendered Christian*. Cleveland, OH: The Pilgrim Press.

Simpson, R.H. (2005) 'How to be fashionably queer: Reminding the Church of the importance of sexual stories.' *Theology & Sexuality 11*, 2, 97–108.

Stonewall School Report (2017) Available at www.stonewall.org.uk/school-report-2017, accessed on 29 July 2019.

Tanis, J. (2003) *Trans-Gendered: Theology, Ministry and Communities of Faith*. Cleveland, OH: The Pilgrim Press.

Taylder, S. (2009) 'Shot from both sides: theology and the woman who isn't quite what she seems.' In M. Althaus-Reid and L. Isherwood (eds) *Trans/Formations*. London: SCM Press.

Thatcher, A. (2011) *God, Sex and Gender: An Introduction.* Chichester: Wiley-Blackwell.

Walker, A.T. (2017/18) *God and the Transgender Debate: What does the Bible Actually Say about Gender Identity?* Epsom: The Good Book Company.

Williams, R. (1979) *The Wound of Knowledge: Christian Spirituality from the New Testament to St John of the Cross.* London: Darton, Longman & Todd.

World Professional Association for Transgender Health (WPATH) (2012) *Standards of Care* (SOC) Version 7. Available at www.wpath.org/publications/soc, accessed on 29 July 2019.

Yarhouse, M. (2015) *Understanding Gender Dysphoria: Navigating Transgender Issues in a Changing Culture.* Downers Grove, IL: Inter-Varisty Press Academic.

Zhou, J., Hofman M., Gooren, L. and Swaab, D. (1995) 'A sex difference in the human brain and its relation to transsexuality.' *Nature 378*, 68–70.

Subject Index

Author Index